SCHOOL-CENTRED MANAGEMENT TRAINING

Mike Wallace is a research fellow at the National Development Centre for Educational Management and Policy at the University of Bristol. He has acted as a consultant and researcher for LEAs, the DES and the School Management Training Task Force. He is currently carrying out research funded by the Economic and Social Research Council and the Leverhulme Trust. Previously he was a teacher in primary and middle schools. His doctoral research was based on action research into his practice as a deputy headteacher. He has published widely on school management training and the management of educational change.

SCHOOL-CENTRED MANAGEMENT TRAINING

MIKE WALLACE

Paul Chapman Publishing Ltd

Paul Chapman Publishing Ltd
144 Liverpool Road
London
N1 1LA

British Library Cataloguing in Publication Data

Wallace, Mike
    School-centred management training. – (Managing
    better schools NDC EMP)
    I. Title   II. Series
    371.200941

    ISBN 1-85396-099-3

Typeset by Inforum Typesetting, Portsmouth
Printed by St. Edmundsbury Press, Bury St. Edmunds
and bound by W.H. Ware, Clevedon, England

CONTENTS

FOREWORD AND ACKNOWLEDGEMENTS

This book has been a long time brewing. Some years ago, as a newly appointed and enthusiastic deputy head, I successfully applied for a place on a locally advertized residential management course for deputies. I had no idea why I got in while fellow deputies who applied did not and was given little idea about what I might be in for. No preparation was required on my part before turning up with eager anticipation on the first day. We received a lecture on the law as it affects schooling, followed by a lecture on management by objectives. Neither topic bore directly upon my concerns at the time which were more to do with establishing credibility with my new colleagues in school. We then spent many hours tackling a simulation exercise which entailed planning the staffing and the curriculum policy for a fictional school. However, this school was in a different phase from those in which participants worked, so the staffing ratios and certain curriculum areas that we were expected to consider in the simulation did not match those in our schools. No evaluation was invited during or after the course.

By the time it was over, I had taken in three compartmented experiences that seemed neither to relate to each other nor to centre upon the pressing problems with which I was concerned in school. Subsequently I learned that the same course was offered to headteachers and to other staff with management responsibility in different sizes of school serving different pupil age ranges. If the needs of participants with different levels of responsibility or experience differed, no account of this possibility appeared to have been taken in offering this all purpose form of learning support. I know now that provision of this kind was not untypical and was widely regarded as acceptable practice at a time when learning support was conceived, in the main, as something that happened outside schools.

While the course had little impact upon my work as a deputy head its – no doubt unintended – impact was to stimulate my efforts since to discover how to provide more effective learning support for staff with managerial responsibility in schools that centred more closely upon their work. As I became more conversant with the ever increasing variety of activities and programmes available I was surprised to realize how many offered all sorts of exciting experiences which covered just about everything else except, seemingly, the one essential: learning support with doing the job itself.

In writing this book it might have been safest to go no further than portraying something of the rich and burgeoning variety of approaches that exist for supporting learning for school management. Readers would then be left to make up their own minds about which activities and programmes to try according to their personal experiences, preferences and beliefs. There are many – often contradictory – views about the most effective forms of learning support. However, it seems likely to be of greater practical help, if more contentious, to offer readers rather more than a directory by giving advice on the basis of such evidence as we have about effective learning support. I have therefore attempted to assess a wide range of activities and programmes according to what we know from relevant research, professional knowledge and theory, and to extrapolate from this knowledge base in offering some guidance about ways of maximizing the effectiveness of learning support. As this knowledge base is not without limits, the analysis and advice offered here must be accepted as being in some degree tentative.

The handbook is aimed at a very wide audience. Readers' background knowledge and experience of providing learning support for managers in schools is likely to vary considerably. My intention is, on the one hand, to offer ideas and guidance for uninitiated readers without blinding them with science; on the other, to offer food for thought to experienced trainers by providing some justification for the principles and practices advocated and through reference to the relevant literature. Whatever their role and experience, I hope that readers will find something of practical value in the book.

I would like to express my thanks to Gordon Bell, whose encouragement helped me to begin this inquiry; to Moyra Bentley, who helped me to sharpen my thinking about the nature of managerial performance and learning; to Ray Bolam, Valerie Hall, Agnes McMahon, David Oldroyd and Cyril Poster, my present and former colleagues at the NDC who have given me so many ideas and learning opportunities; to the trainers and LEA advisers who helped me to learn from their work; and to Angela Allen, June Collins and Joan Moore of the NDC support staff, who sorted out the manuscript after my wordprocessor had finished with it.

Mike Wallace
Bristol
1991

1
INTRODUCTION

Centring on the school

Most headteachers and staff with management responsibility in Britain's schools have never been trained as managers. In many cases they have learned through trial and error in the job, helped perhaps by noting how competent colleagues go about their work. According to surveys by Her Majesty's Inspectors (HMI) the majority of these people perform their management tasks satisfactorily or better. So is management training really necessary?

My argument is that, to become and continue to be an effective manager, it is essential to learn by doing the job. There is no other way. Learning from unplanned experience is, however, haphazard and inefficient. Many learning opportunities will be missed as managers concentrate on getting the job done rather than what they might learn from doing it. The experience of learning through the job can be made less of a trial and risk rather less error if, instead of learning by more or less unconscious osmosis, managers make a sustained commitment to learning by reflection on their job experience coupled with action to improve their performance in the light of their reflection. While teachers aspiring towards management positions and experienced managers faced with new tasks cannot learn to perform effectively without doing the job, they can begin the process through preparatory work. Even the most experienced managers are unlikely to achieve perfection. There is always more to be learned, especially in the present period of radical education reform where new management tasks are required to be undertaken in schools.

Learning for managerial performance may be greatly accelerated if managers do not have to go it alone. Headteachers are in a key position to help themselves and their staff to become more effective managers by fostering the conditions which maximize the possibility of learning through performance of everyday management tasks. A wide range of preparatory and ongoing support is potentially available to help them to make the most of the possibilities for learning. Such support provides structured opportunities for managers to reflect upon their job performance, offers tools for reflection and encourages attempts to improve practice. Yet in the area of education management the potential of many of these strategies has yet to be tapped.

In encouraging those responsible for supporting the learning of managers in schools to extend the range of their strategies in profitable directions, this handbook has a fourfold purpose:

- to establish principles of effective learning support within a management development framework, based upon the evidence of research, professional knowledge and theory;
- to describe a range of strategies for supporting learning which are or may be adapted so that they are consistent with what we know about how managers learn;
- to offer advice on how these approaches may be used effectively within training courses and development programmes based in schools;
- to suggest how evaluation may be carried out with the primary aim of improving learning support activities and programmes.

It is intended for staff in schools with a role in providing learning support for their colleagues and those with a relevant supporting role who are based outside schools. This wide audience thus includes school staff with responsibility for co-ordinating staff development; headteachers, who are responsible for the development of their colleagues; LEA staff with a co-ordination brief for in-service training and initiatives such as the Training and Vocational Education Initiative Extension (TVE), implementation of the National Curriculum, the Local Management of Schools (LMS) and appraisal; teachers' centre leaders; trainers in LEAs and higher education institutions; and independent consultants. Its principal use is as a source of ideas in considering how to broaden the range and improve the effectiveness of school based and external learning support activities and programmes. A variety of activities are described and a framework, backed by what we know from research, professional knowledge and theory, is offered for the design and evaluation of activities and programmes. The performance of management tasks in the job is the starting point and focus for learning support. In this sense the handbook offers a *school-centred* approach to management training.

The work undertaken by the National Development Centre (NDC) underpins the approach advocated here. During the 1980s the NDC was charged by the Department of Education and Science (DES) with the task of promoting effective management training courses for headteachers and senior staff in schools. In 1983 central government made available to LEAs specific funds for regional courses run by providers from higher education institutions. These courses involved either twenty days away from school, with the intention of improving participants' performance as managers, or a one term secondment, designed to train participants as trainers of their colleagues in other schools. At the same time the NDC was set up with the initial brief to monitor, co-ordinate, support, and promote the effectiveness of these courses. The Centre was also given the task of investigating good management training practice in industry and commerce and promoting ideas arising from this study which could be transferred to the sphere of school management training.

It rapidly became apparent that external training courses alone were an inadequate strategy for improving the managerial performance of heads and senior staff across the country. In many companies external training courses formed a small and integral component of a more comprehensive long-term strategy for management development. In the light of this knowledge, work on management development was conducted by the NDC with eight LEAs and a sample of their schools, giving rise to the handbooks for LEAs and for schools in this series. At the same time a wide range of activities for supporting learning was explored (Wallace, 1986a, 1990a) alongside continuing support for providers and LEAs to promote greater integration of training courses within a management development strategy (Wallace, 1988; Wallace and Hall, 1989).

Learning support and educational reform

If governments expect school staff to manage better schools in the 1990s, arguably they deserve better learning support. Many headteachers and staff with management responsibility are likely to perceive themselves as less effective than they would wish in performing many of their present management tasks and those looming on the horizon. In common with many Western countries, the education reform programme currently being implemented by the British government implies that staff must both modify their existing management practice and learn to carry out a multitude of new tasks.

The extent of the learning required is amply illustrated by the range and pace of the innovations for schools in this country which are represented by these reforms. There has been a rapid build-up of central government initiatives through the 1980s which are technically optional but highly resourced. For instance secondary schools have been encouraged to join the Training and Vocational Education Initiative (TVEI) and its extension. Many schools in both sectors have been involved in LEA initiatives stimulated by central government Education Support Grants, which enabled LEAs to bid for extra resources.

Now all mainstream state schools are compelled to implement a controversial programme of central government reforms, many of which are embodied in the 1986 and 1988 Education Acts. First, a national framework of curriculum goals and standards is being established through the National Curriculum and its associated testing procedures, together with the introduction of national conditions of service for staff which stipulate that all teachers may be required to contribute to the management of their school. Second, within this framework decision-making power is being decentralised to the school level through an increase in the powers of governors, the Local Management of Schools (LMS) and the opportunity for staff salaries to be determined locally in part.

This power is being gained at the expense of power hitherto resting with LEAs. They are required to support the introduction of national innovations by managing the provision of related in-service training; collecting information from schools, in many cases through development plans; and devolving an increasing proportion of finances to schools through the LMS budget formula, derived by LEAs within limits defined by central government.

Third, an education marketplace is being created with greater parental choice and competition between schools through open enrolment of pupils, increased representation of parents on governing bodies, publication of aggregated test scores, the possibility of opting out of LEA control and the creation of a limited number of city technology colleges. Fourth, the performance of schools is to be assessed in relation to curriculum goals and standards and other national innovations; schools are required to evaluate the performance of staff through appraisal and LEAs have the duty to inspect their schools, using specified performance indicators.

Devolution to governors of the power to appoint and dismiss staff has influenced the timing of reorganization plans in some LEAs. Changing the age of transfer between phases of schooling enables LEAs to respond to pressure from central government to remove surplus pupil places. After 1993, when governors have full powers under LMS, LEAs will not be able to control the appointment and redeployment of staff, rendering large scale reorganization much more difficult in future.

Other central government policies affect management tasks in schools. Most notable is the local community charge or poll tax whose largest single element, at the time of writing, is a contribution to educational provision. Cuts are sought by elected members in local authorities to avoid being penalized by central government for overspending, or to influence the future voting pattern of the local electorate by keeping down the size of the community charge. A second policy that has affected many schools indirectly is compulsory competitive tendering for local services such as school buildings and grounds maintenance, resulting from the 1988 Local Government Act.

Each of the education reforms entails management tasks of two kinds, some of which will be new to staff: those required to organize its introduction, including associated in-service training support (such as arranging a staff conference on National Curriculum assessment); and the relevant day to day tasks once the change is implemented (for example, the tasks of organizing annual assessment procedures within the National Curriculum). The combination of all the reforms and other influential policies, alongside any innovations for schools originating with the LEA or the schools themselves, gives rise to a third set of management tasks entailed in managing all innovations and ongoing work simultaneously. Strategic planning and monitoring progress with innovations are examples of these tasks (see Wallace, 1991).

Given the scale and pace of change, Bolam (1989) has suggested that heavy reliance will have to be placed upon provision for these managers of short conferences and workshops of no more than a few days. An NDC survey of provision by higher education institutions immediately prior to the Education Reform Act (Wallace, 1988) implied that LEAs were already sacrificing opportunities for in depth study in order to cover the waterfront by supporting short, necessarily more superficial courses targeted at a larger number of participants. A major effort is being made to raise school managers' awareness and to brief them about the implementation of the reforms through the familiar 'cascade' approach to training. Commonly, a national agency promotes awareness-raising through national conferences and materials aimed at LEA staff who, in their turn, make equivalent arrangements for school staff, who then organize school based events. What these useful occasions for providing information cannot easily achieve is to provide opportunities for practising the skills involved in actually performing the new management tasks.

Assuming that the present scope and pace of change will continue in the coming years, it is becoming increasingly imperative that support for school managers reaches the parts that cascade training does not reach. First, we should be aiming to ensure that existing approaches to school management training and other forms of learning support are as effective as possible. Second, we should be looking for new ways of supporting managers which will help them to make effective use of their chance to learn through experience with their new tasks.

Long term needs

The case seems obvious for a level of learning support that matches the number and complexity of new management tasks following from reform programmes. However this is not the whole story; there are other sources of need. Bolam (1982a) has identified the following purposes for in-service activities aimed at professional development.

(1) Improving the professional knowledge, skills and performance of the whole school staff or a group of staff (e.g. through a school based course on implementing the National Curriculum and its assessment within each subject area intended for all staff with curriculum responsibility in a primary school). Initiatives may originate with central government, as in the case of current education reforms, with LEAs or with schools. Staff may be required to undergo training whether they see the need or not.
(2) Improving the professional knowledge, skills and performance of an individual (e.g. through an induction programme for a new headteacher).
(3) Extending the experience of an individual for career development or promotion purposes (e.g. through an external training course about preparation for headship intended for deputy heads).
(4) Developing the professional knowledge and understanding of an individual (e.g. through a Master's degree course in education management).
(5) Extending the personal or general education of an individual (e.g. through an Open University course in subjects other than education and not directly related to teaching or the management of schools).

Sources of need related to school management other than purpose one (staff or group performance), which has received such heavy emphasis as a result of central government reforms, are likely to be considered as legitimate candidates for support. Needs arise from the potential for individuals to improve their performance of existing tasks in their present job (purpose two); their aspiration to further their career by preparing to perform new tasks in a new job (purpose three); and their wish to increase their personal professional knowledge about educational management so as to inform their work in school (purpose four). Purpose five – personal education – is generally seen as an individual's responsibility even if it has an indirect spin-off for management, as in the case of, say, a degree course in psychology which includes a focus upon group dynamics.

A national survey of school management development and training provision was undertaken at the time when the 1988 Education Reform Act was passed (Wallace and Hall, 1989). This study indicated that systematic support for the longer term development of heads and senior staff, which the majority of LEAs had built up in the previous few years, had in many cases been swamped by the immediate and urgent need to give staff adequate preparation for the effective implementation of the reforms. Especially marked was the decline in support for long award-bearing courses (serving purpose four) offered almost exclusively by higher education institutions. If we are to continue the good work of the 1980s in laying the foundations for schools to be managed by well qualified and competent staff in the 1990s, we must accept that school staff are entitled to some measure of support in improving their existing performance, especially when starting a new job, in developing their career, and in deepening their understanding of their world of work.

The rationale for long educational courses is not confined to their intrinsic value in enhancing individuals' job satisfaction by raising their awareness through in depth professional study. In so far as heads and senior staff should be encouraged to act as professionals who are critically concerned to do the right things, as opposed to mere technicians who do things right as dictated by others, it is essential that they are supported in articulating, reflecting upon and justifying their beliefs and values. Bolam (1990) argues that professionals make relatively autonomous judgements in carrying out their tasks according to the perceived needs of their clients. Therefore professional development should aim to inform these judgements through consideration of their professional and educational values.

It is not self-evident what effective performance of management tasks actually means. One person's democratic style is another's indecision; one person's leading from the front is another's dictatorship. School management is about people and the values they hold about how they should treat each other. There may be intrinsic value for staff in engaging in the managerial tasks which are necessary to co-ordinate their work, but management is fundamentally a means towards the end of bringing about effective teaching and learning for pupils' education. People hold different values about education, teaching and management. It is important that school managers attempt to improve their performance of management tasks in a way which is consistent with their articulated professional, managerial and educational values. Part of the business of learning to be an effective manager is connected with making explicit, justifying and acting in accordance with these values. They should be backed by the results of research and professional experience, and not be simply a reflection of idiosyncratic views. On the basis of this argument there is a case for a range of strategies for learning support. These strategies should include in depth study that is linked to practice in school and enhances participants' ability to make informed judgements in carrying out their management tasks.

In sum, strategies for redressing the balance of learning support are required if we are to pave the way for effective management of schools in the future. Many of those who will be the headteachers of the twenty-first century are in the education profession now and would benefit from greater support as they shoulder increasing management responsibility.

Extending access and increasing effectiveness

The 1980s witnessed a concerted effort on the part of central government to increase the provision of management training for schools. Valuable though this effort has been, the majority of current heads and senior staff are likely to have received little or none of this training. While up to date figures are not available, an indication of the scale of management training is suggested by the estimate that during the period of the government's special funding initiative from 1983 to 1987 about 6,000 heads and senior staff received training amounting to at least twenty days (Wallace, 1988). The DES has since continued to accord high priority to management development and training under the LEA Training Grants Scheme and its successor, Grants for Education Support and Training. Funds have remained at a broadly equivalent level, with the emphasis increasingly turning towards management tasks implied by reforms such as LMS.

There are estimated to be about 25,000 headteachers, 30,000 deputy heads, and another 70,000 staff with substantial management responsibility in England and Wales (McMahon and Bolam, 1990a), plus those who aspire towards these roles. Since all teachers participate in the management of their school, whether as managers or the managed, they all contribute to management to some extent. If, however, we accept that training should be targeted on those with the greatest management responsibility, we are talking of around 130,000 heads and senior staff. Significant, centrally funded training appears likely to reach no more than a very small percentage of this number in any year. Of course other forms of learning support exist, including the short awareness-raising workshops mentioned above, open or distance learning packages, and long award-bearing courses. Yet it is unclear how effective they are and to what extent they reach the target group across the country.

There is a long tradition of management training courses in Britain, going back twenty years or more. A national survey of professional development provision for heads and senior staff over a decade ago (Hughes, Carter and Fidler, 1981) suggested that courses of various lengths were virtually the sole form of learning support. We have some more recent knowledge of the good and the bad news relating to the one term and twenty day courses mounted under the special funding initiative, which gives an idea of the possibilities for improving this type of training. Monitoring visits to a sample of these courses in 1987 (see Wallace, 1988) suggested that, while the courses themselves were generally much appreciated by the participants, they were frequently experienced as a bolt-on extra, divorced in some ways from participants' practice in school. Some common difficulties concerned the lack of a close partnership between LEAs, which sponsored the courses, providers from higher education institutions who delivered them, and the participants. For example, many participants did not know why they had been selected: whether as a remedy for poor performance or a boost to existing competence. Other difficulties related to some course content and methods which did not appear to participants to be of intrinsic interest, challenging or relevant to their work with colleagues in school.

These findings confirmed the significance of issues connected with selection and preparation of participants and follow-up in school which were highlighted in a study of external management training courses commissioned by the DES (Bailey, 1987). Many of the problems identified in these studies are the hardy perennials of external training courses for teachers (see Rudduck, 1981), especially difficulty with forging a link between the course experience and participants' practice in school (see also Wallace, 1986b), and therefore seem unlikely to have been weeded out of the present range of training provision. There is probably room to make external training courses more effective by attending both to the activities they entail and to the surrounding processes which ensure that the experience challenges and supports participants in improving their job performance.

In recent years many LEAs have devolved a considerable proportion of their funds for in-service training to schools and, given current central government pressure upon LEAs, this trend seems likely to continue. Within the conditions of service for teachers imposed by the government in 1987, five days each year are available to staff when the pupils do not attend, designed to facilitate a variety of initiatives originating in schools to support the development of staff. Potentially, staff with management responsibility have an increasing number of opportunities to receive development support organized at the level of the school. There is thus a good case for exploring a wide range of activities which may support learning, whether or not they are incorporated within a course.

An unintended and widespread consequence of the dramatic increase in in-service training for both management and staff development has been disruption for pupils' classwork. This problem has been caused by the frequent absence of teachers who are attending training elsewhere and the difficulty faced by many schools in procuring adequate supply cover on a regular basis (HMI, 1989; DES, 1989). According to a recent national survey of LEAs (Brown and Earley, 1990) the response has been twofold. Strategies have been developed by LEAs to improve the availability of supply cover so that teachers may be released, which has alleviated shortages to a limited extent. Schools have increasingly turned to arrangements for in-service training based in school which does not require cover, including:

- making use of the five annual non-contact days for in-service training;
- scheduling activities outside the school day but during directed time;
- creative timetabling, especially in larger schools, where staff non-contact time can be adjusted to support teachers taking part in in-service training;
- arranging voluntary activities outside directed time;
- increasing the use of distance learning materials;
- enabling external support teachers to work alongside teachers in their classrooms.

Thus one reason for increasing the use of management development activities which do not require staff to be released from their regular teaching commitment is to avoid disruption for pupils.

Messages from the School Management Task Force

A School Management Task Force was set up by central government in 1989. Its remit is to review existing training provision and to assist LEAs and providers of training in the public and private sectors in ensuring adequate provision of management development and training opportunities for heads and senior staff in schools. Wide consultation by members of the Task Force with interested parties inside and outside education has resulted in the publication of its report (DES, 1990) which includes the following important messages for the improvement of learning support:

- the development of school managers should be based upon their commitment to developing themselves by learning through reflective practice in their normal job;
- they are entitled to expect some support which, if it is to be widely accessible at a feasible cost, must centre upon supervision and feedback in school and activities near the school, coupled with opportunities for career development through carrying out new tasks;
- this support should be complemented by the provision of external training experiences, including open learning, which employ experiential methods focusing upon participants' work in school and encourage experimentation in the job;
- opportunities for development should be available at the stage of induction into all senior management posts;
- equal opportunities for development should be provided at all levels of management;

- co-ordinated effort is required between heads and their staff, LEAs, and public and private sector providers to ensure coherence of provision to meet a balance of identified individual and corporate development needs;
- LEAs may benefit from economies of scale, especially for external training courses, by operating as regional groups.

Thus the Task Force's approach to learning support for school managers is founded upon self help, backed by a range of opportunities to stimulate and enhance what may be learned simply by doing the job. An integral part of the headteachers' role is to create conditions conducive to the learning of staff with and aspiring towards management responsibility. Staff have a complementary responsibility to help their colleagues to learn through their work as managers. Creating jobs that are manageable, challenging and rewarding within an environment in which staff are encouraged to experiment in the job and to support the learning of their colleagues are therefore key elements in managing school-centred management development. In subsequent chapters these messages will be amplified in considering how to get the best from a range of approaches to learning support. However, the main emphasis will be placed upon the design and evaluation of activities that directly support learning for job performance, rather than upon the process of creating favourable conditions for learning through, say, job design or staff appraisal.

Key terms relating to management development and training

It is important to clarify at the outset the main terms used in the remaining chapters so that readers may find a path through the jargon jungle. *Management* is taken to mean carrying out tasks, additional to teaching, which are achieved with and through other adults in school. A co-ordinated approach to improving management is *management development*, a part of staff development. It embraces the dynamic process of organizing the planned development of individuals and groups in learning to perform management tasks more skilfully so that the school is more effective, ultimately, in giving pupils a worthwhile, consistent and progressive educational experience. In more detail, the process of management development entails developing a policy; identifying individual, group and whole staff needs; establishing priorities among these needs; and planning, resourcing, implementing and evaluating a programme of activities to meet priority needs. In this handbook we will focus mainly upon programmes of activities to meet needs. (For further information on organizing and supporting management development for schools at LEA level see McMahon and Bolam, 1990a; on the process at school level see McMahon and Bolam, 1990b and 1990c; and on the process of managing staff development at school level see Oldroyd and Hall, 1991a; Wallace, 1990b.)

The NDC's formal working definition of management development is 'the process whereby the management function of an organization is performed with

increasing effectiveness'. This definition highlights how management development is concerned with overall managerial effectiveness – not just the development of individuals, and encompasses a range of approaches to learning support
– not just external training courses. Within the process of management development it is helpful to distinguish three broad components:

(1) *Management training* to meet development needs – short conferences,
    courses and workshops that focus upon specific practical information and
    skills required for job performance, that seldom lead to a qualification or
    award and may be organized by LEAs, schools or trainers from higher
    education or elsewhere.
(2) *Management education* to meet development needs – secondments, fellow-
    ships and long, external courses involving full or part time study, aimed at
    improving overall competence through increasing general understanding,
    often emphasizing research and theoretical knowledge relevant to educa-
    tional management and its policy context, and leading to higher education
    and professional qualifications (e.g. a Master's degree).
(3) *Management support* – a range of managerial procedures and activities for
    deploying staff (e.g. staff selection, planned succession); identifying needs
    (e.g. appraisal, school review); identifying priorities for meeting needs (e.g.
    reference to an equal opportunities policy); meeting development needs
    (e.g. rotation of jobs, allocation of additional responsibilities); and evaluat-
    ing learning (e.g. monitoring and feedback arrangements).

Since this handbook is about methods of learning support to meet management
development needs we will focus mainly upon training and those management
support procedures for meeting development needs in school, with some reference
to education. The building blocks of learning support are planned *activities*, which
vary from the simple (e.g. observing the headteacher going through the morning
post) to the complex (e.g. an in-service training day for all staff on team building).
Activities may be combined into a *programme* (e.g. an external training course
which includes observation of colleagues as they carry out their management tasks in
school). Programmes of activities may include components of training, education
and management support. Reference will also be made to the *process of managing
learning support* activities and programmes within the wider framework of management development, with special emphasis upon design and evaluation issues.

Activities and programmes generally take place in one of three situations:

● *on the job* – in participants' schools as part of their performance of their
  management tasks;
● *close to the job* – within participants' or other schools but not directly related
  to their own performance in post;
● *off the job* – in a setting both institutionally and geographically separated
  from participants' schools.

While management training and education programmes have traditionally been located off the job, it is possible to include both close to the job and on the job activities within them. Similarly learning support activities and programmes taking place on the job may be supplemented by close to the job and off the job activities. A key planning issue for co-ordinators in school and external trainers is to think creatively about how most effectively to meet identified management development needs within the resources that are likely to be available. It is important to avoid limiting consideration about learning support programmes to one or other of the traditionally separate components of training, education and those aspects of management support intended to meet development needs.

Arrangement of the remaining chapters

At the risk of seeming presumptuous, here is a word of advice about how to get the most from this handbook. The content that is likely to be of most immediate interest is the description of activities for supporting managers' learning. However, activities are unlikely to be effective and, indeed, some may well prove disastrous unless, first, learning needs are identified before alighting upon a particular activity; second, activities are selected which stand a good chance of meeting these needs; and third, they are carefully planned and organized to guard against any risk of things going wrong. The activities which get to the heart of improving management performance are often the ones which are potentially the most threatening (often referred to as 'high gain, high strain'). Moreover, their effectiveness is easily lost if they are diluted by, say, using some elements which are straighforward or fun to do while dropping others.

It is important to think about the principles of learning, learning support and organization that underpin activities, to consider how to design effective programmes of learning support, and to explore how they may be integrated within the continual process of management development for school staff, rather than appearing as an isolated 'bolt on' event. Readers are likely to get most from this handbook if they refer to the chapters which deal with these issues as well as glancing at the activities themselves.

Chapter 2 draws upon professional knowledge from the NDC's work on management training and elsewhere, relevant research and learning theory in developing an account of managerial performance and learning. Against this backdrop, general principles are identified as a grounding for the design of effective learning support activities and programmes.

Chapter 3 describes activities and Chapter 4 describes sets of activities designed as programmes for learning support which look promising according to the principles identified in the previous chapter. They are drawn from experience of learning support inside and outside education. For each activity or programme an account of the main features is given, the potential impact upon managerial performance is considered, planning and design issues are raised, and some possible uses are suggested.

Chapter 5 discusses the design of programmes and encourages readers to think creatively about combinations of on the job, close to the job and off the job activities. Consideration is given to the process of managing learning support programmes; key steps in programme design, implementation, monitoring and adjustment; and initial planning for evaluation of the quality of the experience and its impact. A sequence of design steps is explored in detail. Chapter 6 consists of a brief description of a variety of programmes with a commentary on each related to the design steps outlined in the previous chapter.

In Chapter 7 we focus upon the main evaluation tasks, picking up the process of managing programme evaluation from the introduction in Chapter 5 and exploring design issues in greater detail. The integration of evaluation with programme management is emphasized by addressing the preparatory tasks connected with evaluations that are part of programme management (Chapter 5) and subsequently considering the tasks for which evaluators are responsible within the framework of programme management (Chapter 7).

Chapter 8 briefly considers the process of managing activities and programmes to meet needs within a wider management development framework. Emphasis is placed upon linkages with the process of management development, including matching activities and programmes with prospective participants' needs. Finally, it is suggested that improving learning support for managers in schools should proceed by a process of incremental change.

Personal experience of learning support

One important source of evidence about effective learning support is professional knowledge: a distillation of the experience of those associated with supporting the learning of adults in mid-career. Most readers will have received learning support, probably in the form of a training course of some kind, during their professional career. Before launching into a consideration of what makes for effective learning support in Chapter 2, a useful preliminary task may be to reflect upon this personal experience. Readers may then connect their personal professional knowledge, born of experience as a participant in learning support activities and programmes, to the evidence presented later.

The questionnaire in Figure 1.1 highlights some components of learning support which research, professional knowledge and theory suggest are effective in helping individuals to improve their job performance. In the first activity readers are invited to consider which components were present in a learning support experience which they found effective in promoting their job related learning. In the second activity the components of an ineffective learning support experience are considered. Finally the components of the two experiences are compared to identify which components appear to have been particularly significant in promoting readers' professional learning.

Some of the components listed in Figure 1.1 will be much easier to put into

Activity 1

Think of the learning support experience of up to one term in length that has been most effective in helping you to improve some aspect of the performance of your present or a previous job.

Please fill in the checklist below.

For each statement put a tick in the box on the left hand side if it applied to your experience or a cross if it did not.

	Activity 1 ✓ or X	Activity 2 ✓ or X
1. Was the learning support relevant to your learning needs which had previously been identified?		
2. Did you know why you were being given the opportunity to have this particular experience?		
3. Did you make any commitment beforehand that you would attempt to learn as much as you could from the experience?		
4. Were any of your colleagues in school involved as participants in the same experience?		
5. Were you given any help with preparation for the experience?		
6. Were you clear how the activities were intended to help you improve your job performance?		
7. Did you have any degree of choice about how you were to learn to carry out new tasks or techniques?		
8. Were the activities varied?		
9. Was a description given of the new tasks or techniques you were learning to carry out?		
10. Were these tasks or techniques explained to you?		
11. Was any demonstration given to provide you with a good example of these tasks or techniques in use in the workplace?		
12. Did you have opportunities to talk with other participants about what you were learning?		
13. Were you able to practise using these tasks or techniques before you tried them out in the workplace?		
14. Were you given feedback on your performance of these tasks or techniques that you were practising?		

	Activity 1 √ or X	Activity 2 √ or X
15. Was any obligation on your part made clear to you to put into practice what you were learning and to share it with colleagues in your workplace?		
16. Were you given opportunities to try out the new tasks or techniques in your normal job in school with feedback on your performance?		
17. Were you given any follow-up coaching or extra tuition to help you improve your performance of these tasks or techniques in the in the workplace?		
18. Were you encouraged to plan relevant action in your workplace after the experience was over?		
19. Did you have an opportunity after the experience to share what you had learned with colleagues in your school or other schools?		
20. Did you have opportunities during the experience to give your opinion on how well it was meeting your needs and about any improvements that could be put into effect before the end of the experience?		
21. Did you have an opportunity to evaluate the experience after it was over?		

Add up your ticks and crosses to give your total score:

Activity 1: ....ticks ....crosses

Research and general practical experience suggest that learning support experience which is effective in improving job performance should ideally include **all** the components implied in these questions. So, the more ticks you had, the more effective the experience was likely to be.

Activity 2

Think of the learning support experience of up to one term in length that has been **least** effective in helping you to improve some aspect of the **performance** of your present or previous job. Fill in the checklist as before but place a tick or cross in each right hand box. Add up your ticks and crosses to give your total score:

Activity 2: ....ticks ....crosses

If research and general practical experience match your personal experience, you will have fewer ticks than in Activity 1. Compare the components for which you put a tick in Activity 1 with those for Activity 2.

Activity 3

Consider which components of learning support you think are most important for improving job performance and why.

Figure 1.1: What is effective learning support?

place than others. For example, it is usually a simple matter to provide variation within activities so as to sustain participants' interest. On the other hand, it may be more difficult to provide for on the job coaching. Components also vary widely in the contribution they make to effective learning for job performance. On the job coaching, as we shall see, is potentially a far more powerful form of support than providing variety within activities. One of Murphy's Laws of Learning Support seems to be that the most effective components tend to be costly. Let us now turn to the evidence from which the checklist was derived.

2

ESTABLISHING PRINCIPLES OF
LEARNING SUPPORT

What works – as far as we know

This chapter begins with a look at what is known from professional experience, research, and theory building about effective learning support for school managers. While not comprehensive, the review provides sufficient evidence and theoretical ideas for a model of managerial performance and learning to be put forward as the basis for identifying some general principles of learning support.

First, however, the bad news: this knowledge base is neither as comprehensive nor as robust as ideally it should be. There is little really hard evidence – although much practical experience and armchair theorizing – underpinning the considerable consensus that, as the Task Force report implies, now exists over what works. Little research has been carried out on how school managers learn to achieve their tasks in school. Evaluation of education and training for school managers has tended to stop at assessing the quality of the course experience, rather than attempting to measure the impact on participants' performance – let alone the indirect impact upon the experience of pupils.

It is difficult, and therefore costly, to provide reliable evidence through research or evaluation. There is a series of links between a learning support activity, changes in managers' behaviour, their impact on the behaviour and attitudes of colleagues, and the impact of colleagues' behaviour upon pupils' learning. It is no simple matter to demonstrate that changes in pupils' learning are the result of a manager's experience of learning support, rather than a host of other factors such as the work of a gifted teacher or pupils' intrinsic interest in a particular topic. Much adult learning and associated teaching theory, including the influential work by Schon (1983, 1987) to be discussed later, appears to have been developed largely through reflection on professional experience and, while it offers a general perspective within which to plan learning support it appears not to have been rigorously tested by subsequent research.

Now the good news: professional knowledge of learning support for school managers has expanded internationally throughout the last decade (e.g. Esp, 1983; Buckley, 1985; Murphy and Hallinger, 1987; Poster and Day, 1988) as experience of an increasing variety of activities has grown. Some research has been carried out in the related fields of in-service training for teachers and management training outside the education sector. This research appears to have important implications for the field of school management training, but it is important to bear in mind that it is uncertain how far we may safely extrapolate from work in other areas. Evaluations of school management training courses do provide information upon participants' judgements of the course experience and, in some cases, their report about its impact on their management practice. While there may be gaps in this professional knowledge and research, the experience and evidence we have points in broadly the same direction. Emerging theory about adult professional learning and training for job performance is generally consistent with this professional knowledge and research. Let us explore how examples of this work suggest a coherent set of messages for learning support.

From imparting knowledge to enhancing performance

There is a long tradition of management education for heads and senior staff in the form of long courses (see Hughes *et al*, 1981) based in higher education and, more recently, independent institutions. Participants are generally presented with a menu of research and theoretical knowledge about school management and its wider social and political context. Their understanding and ability to reflect critically upon this knowledge is assessed, rather than their performance in the job. It is widely assumed that practice in school may be influenced in so far as participants' increased awareness and analytical skills will sharpen their thinking and influence their attempt to match their articulated educational and managerial values with their actions. The primary aim is to educate individuals about the job with a view to informing their work rather than to train them in specific skills of job performance. Increasing experimentation in recent years has resulted from changing arrangements for funding in-service training, a concern to improve access, pressure to accredit learning, and an interest in relating long courses to participants' practice. Initiatives include part-time study, modular courses, distance learning, and projects based in school whose reports are assessed.

There is an equally long tradition of shorter management training courses where, increasingly, the attempt is made to link the course experience closely with participants' performance in the job. Research into curriculum courses for teachers (Rudduck, 1981) revealed a 'casualness of purpose' among some participants who chose from a menu of courses on offer according to their interest, rather than a development need related to their job. Participants were generally critical of courses whose content was not perceived to be relevant or did not provide help with their day to day problems in school.

During the 1970s alternatives to a menu of externally provided courses were developed to bridge the commonly experienced gap between course content and participants' needs. For example, school based in-service training was advocated as a more effective way of meeting individual needs arising from specific teaching and organizational problems (Warwick, 1975). A synthesis of school and course based approaches was incorporated in school focused in-service training. Training needs would be identified in relation to tasks being performed, a range of strategies including school based activities and external courses would be employed to meet these needs, and the activities would be evaluated (Henderson, 1979; Bolam, 1982b).

This process of managing training to meet development needs is consistent with the findings of a small-scale study of management training in industry and commerce carried out by Ballinger (1984). The most effective form of training was reported to involve negotiating a learning contract between the manager, the senior manager and the company trainer. On the job training in the workplace was complemented by close to the job training with the support of the senior manager, or off the job training in specific skills. External courses were little used as they were regarded as expensive and ineffective in meeting job related needs. At this time the performance related learning of managers outside education was increasingly coming to be understood as centred in their day to day work (e.g. Mumford, 1980; Stuart, 1983; Davies and Easterby-Smith, 1984).

Linking an external course with participants' professional experience and development needs has proved to be an important issue in school management training. Course monitoring by the NDC indicated that, where participants were unclear about the criteria for their selection or were given no preparatory tasks that encouraged them to reflect upon their practice, they frequently had difficulty at first in bridging the gap between the course content and their job experience and concerns. A clear message from this work is that learning support efforts should ideally take each participant's job experience as a starting point.

It seems equally important to create a favourable climate where it is possible to build upon that experience through learning support activities which maintain relevance to the job while providing a challenge, sustain interest and offer guidance with implementing changes in practice. This message is reflected in activities perceived as effective by participants on the courses monitored by the NDC, including:

- negotiation of a learning agreement;
- a preparatory visit from the course organizer to participants' schools;
- a modular structure spread over several months, with opportunities to implement in school what had been learned on the course;
- attendance by two or more participants from the same school who worked together on a project in school;
- on the job activities such as monitoring the use of time during the school day;

- a residential period involving team building activities early on so that participants could build the mutual trust needed to share their real concerns relating to their job;
- close to the job activities including school visits or observing another participant in school;
- opportunities to share and solve their school management problems using the experience and advice of other participants;
- stimulating lectures which led participants to question their assumptions while offering guidelines for action in school;
- practice of key skills, such as conducting an appraisal interview, in a safe setting with feedback;
- follow-up activities such as establishing a network of present and past participants.

Mind the gap: transfer of learning

The flipside of taking participants' job experience as a starting point is to finish by ensuring that the learning within an activity becomes an integral part of their job performance. A longstanding concern of trainers has been the gap between what is learned on an external course and changing performance in the job. As Glatter (1972) pointed out long ago, where one person from a school attends a course, changes in job performance are likely to affect the colleagues with and through whom management tasks are carried out. Since they will not have shared the training experience colleagues may not perceive the value of these changes and may therefore resist them. On the basis of extensive experience of learning support for managers outside education, Stuart and Binsted (1981) argue that learning support activities should be designed to ensure that learners perceive them to have links with and relevance for their experiences at work. Where learners do not perceive this connection their learning will be meaningful only in the setting of the activity. Conversely, transfer of learning is favoured where participants perceive that the content, the process or the context of the activity relate closely to their job experience.

However there is more to bridging the gap between a learning support experience and the job than perceived linkage. A deeper problem lies in the distinction revealed by research between course based learning and learning to integrate new behaviour into job performance. In their work as commercial trainers Rackham and Morgan (1977) found that managers have to learn to perform new skills in the specific context of their use, rather than first acquiring skills that can then be applied in any situation without further learning. An investigation conducted by Huczynski and Lewis (1980) into the learning transfer process in management training measured the impact upon participants' practice of two taught courses with specific objectives. The single most important factor influencing transfer was the degree to which participants had discussed the training with senior managers in relation to their needs and had been supported in trying out in the workplace what they had learned on the course. These examples indicate that transfer of learning may require additional learning. Although we know that many people do learn to become effective managers with learning support that does not reach into the workplace or without any form of help, there is strong evidence that learning may be greatly enhanced by on the job support.

The rigorous and extensive research on in-service training for teachers carried out by Joyce and Showers (1980, 1988) suggests how transfer of learning may be promoted. The focus of the training was complex teaching methods such as helping pupils to increase their capacity for critical thinking. The researchers identified the different components of training and their combinations which led to different outcomes for those being trained. Table 2.1 summarizes their findings.

Table 2.1:   Training components, their combinations and impact on job performance

(based on Joyce and Showers, 1988)

Training components and the combinations	Impact on job performance		
	Knowledge	Skill	Transfer of training
Theory	Low	Low	Nil
Theory, demonstration	Medium	Medium	Nil
Theory, demonstration and practice	High	Medium	Nil
Theory, demonstration, practice and feedback	High	Medium	Low
Theory, demonstration, practice, feedback and coaching	High	High	High

Joyce and Showers distinguished between the knowledge and skill required for mechanistic use of what had been learned through training in the job and its creative integration into participants' repertoire of teaching strategies, for which they reserved the label 'transfer of training'. The results of this research form the basis of their model of training for job performance.

A combination of all five training components appears most likely to result in effective integration of new skills or the refinement of existing ones within participants' repertoire. Presentation of the theory or rationale for, say, a new teaching method will raise participants' awareness and an additional demonstration of the method in use, perhaps by means of a video, will give them the more detailed understanding necessary to perform the skills involved. Opportunities to practise the method in the training situation, possibly through a simulation exercise, will enhance skill performance in the training setting. However, there is likely to be little transfer of the training into participants' practice as teachers.

The skills may be employed mechanically but are unlikely to be deployed creatively and appropriately as an integral part of participants' repertoire. In many cases the skills are soon lost as few participants practise them regularly without the provision of further support. When opportunities for constructive, factual feedback are given on participants' performance while practising the method in the training session, there is generally some transfer of training: the new skills are often eventually used regularly in the classroom, they are deployed appropriately for the situation in hand and they are integrated with the existing repertoire.

The additional training component of coaching in the job situation by colleagues who have also received training is particularly powerful in promoting transfer. Coaching implies that teachers observe each other in the classroom and give mutual feedback to see how far the skills are being practised; they examine the appropriate use of the teaching strategy; and they engage in collaborative problem solving and action planning sessions. A valuable spin off from this way of working is the collaborative relationships and mutual encouragement it tends to generate among teachers in the same school (Showers, 1985).

Several important messages arise from this work with implications for training focused upon job performance:

- a combination of didactic and practical activities is required – neither lectures about school management practice, nor videos from distance learning packages, nor activities drawing exclusively upon participants' experience are sufficient on their own;
- performing skilfully in the job consists of more than the sum of discrete elements of knowledge and skills that may be learned in the training setting;
- the learning entailed in improving job performance includes a component which is distinct both from what may be learned cognitively through lectures and demonstrations and what may be learned through the experience of performance and feedback in the training setting;
- a positive attitude towards transfer of learning is fostered through the emotional support offered by peers who are also learning the same practice;
- transfer of learning is greatly enhanced not merely by feedback on participants' performance, both in the training and job settings, but by the guidance to be gained from on the job coaching. In other words, follow-up support that gets to the heart of the job is a key to transfer of learning.

The relevance of these findings to school management is strongly supported by professional experience with school management training courses. For example, Bailey (1987) reports on a range of activities conceived as part of the course experience which provide support for individual work and opportunities for collaboration with colleagues to improve job performance.

Research by Leithwood and Montgomery (1986) on the performance of elementary school principals (headteachers) gives us a clue as to what is distinctive about school managers' job performance in comparison with performance in a training setting. While their work was based more upon informed opinion than upon observation of behaviour in the job, a high degree of consensus amongst informants was found about how more or less effective principals operate. Leithwood and Montgomery developed a profile of growth in principal effectiveness. Principals operating at the highest level engaged in a problem solving approach to the job in which they investigated the consequences of their actions, questioned their assumptions and experimented in the light of their reflection. Subsequently Leithwood and Steger (1989) carried out a small scale study of principals' problem solving strategies by inviting them to talk through how they would approach a range of more or less highly structured job related problems. When faced with ill-structured problems the principals identified as most effective used more sophisticated and penetrative strategies than their more typical peers. These findings are consistent with emerging theory about adult growth which suggests that individuals identified as having reached a higher stage of development operate in a more complex manner, possess a wider repertoire of behavioural skills, perceive problems more broadly and can respond more effectively to the needs of others (Pitner, 1987).

Management situations in school may be more complex and therefore more problematic to deal with than the artificially simplified situations common in training settings where skills are practised. The experience of, say, strategic planning within a simulation of a school or the experience of team building within an outdoor training exercise may be significantly different from strategic planning or building a team with colleagues in the job situation. One key difference is that the stakes are considerably higher in school – the consequences of mistakes might be serious!

Research into management training conducted by Burgoyne and Stuart (1977) provides evidence that learning support should ideally include help with solving the problems of performance in the job. They found an association between involving participants in solving management problems requiring action in the job situation and the development of their managerial problem solving skills. On the other hand, management problems presented via simulations were discovered to be less effective, providing backing for the contention that the experience of active learning off the job is not the real thing – it is no more than preparation for learning that still has to take place. Transfer of learning implies additional learning within the problematic setting of the job.

Experiential learning and reflective practice

As we have seen, professional knowledge and research over recent years has reinforced the case for grounding learning support in participants' job experience rather than trainers' wealth of more or less abstract knowledge relevant to the job. Efforts to provide explanations of these findings which may guide attempts to design approaches to learning support have been made through the development of models and theories of learning. Three of the most influential theories are briefly addressed here. All draw upon the philosophy of John Dewey. (For a more comprehensive exposition of theories of learning and training see Rodwell, 1986.)

Knowles (1984) distinguishes adult learning – which he refers to as andragogy – from children's learning. Andragogy is based upon the assumptions that adults are self-directed, have a reservoir of experiences to draw upon, learn what is necessary for them to perform their social roles and are problem centred in their approach to learning. These characteristics of adult learners imply that their teachers should act as facilitators whereas teachers of children are purveyors of knowledge. The assumptions of this theory have been criticized as overly simplistic (e.g. Day and Baskett, 1982). Adults and children vary in the amount of direction they need or request; they vary in the degree to which they avoid learning what is necessary for them to perform their social roles; and teachers of adults and children may employ didactic and facilitation approaches. Nevertheless the theory does point to the gradual accumulation of experience from childhood to adulthood which forms the platform for further learning and to the common experience that many managers are greatly interested in learning to solve problems related to their job roles.

An arguably more significant contribution to our understanding of job related learning has been provided by Kolb (1984), whose theory of experiential learning is conceived as a four stage cycle, as shown in Figure 2.1.

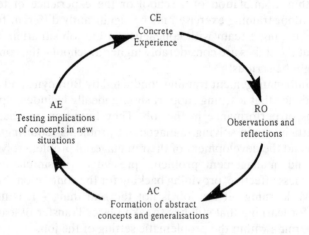

Figure 2.1:   Kolb's Experiential Learning Model

Immediate concrete experience is viewed as the basis for observation and reflection. The observations are assimilated into an idea, image or theory from which implications for future action may be derived. These implications, hunches or hypotheses then guide action to create new concrete experiences. Learners require the skills to immerse themselves openly in new experiences (CE), to reflect upon these experiences (RO), to integrate these observations into more abstract conceptual schemes or theories (AC), to use these theories to guide decision-making and experimental action to solve problems (AE), leading to new experiences. Kolb argues that effective learning from experience entails the complete cycle which, however, is not as simple as it may appear.

Learners must operate on two dimensions which consist of polar opposites. The concrete-abstract dimension (CE-AC) requires them to be open to a new experience while simultaneously being detached enough to gain an overview and plan ahead. The reflective-experimental dimension (RO-AE) requires both active experimentation and reflective observation. Research into how far the cycle was reflected in individuals' learning behaviour revealed wide variation, commonly being biased towards one or more parts of the cycle. Kolb claims that individuals' preferred learning styles may become more effective if they are more balanced, reflecting the complete cycle. This account provides an explanation for the combination of didactic and practical training activities that Joyce and Showers demonstrated to promote the learning of complex teaching skills. Presentation of theory and demonstration of good teaching according to the theory give a basis for initial conceptualizing and observation while practice, feedback and coaching provide opportunities for experiment, concrete experience and reflection, using the concepts of the theory. Like andragogy, experiential learning also points to the centrality of participants' experience, whether in the training situation or in the job. Practical implications of this theory include diagnosing the bias in individuals' learning styles and fostering more balanced learning habits.

However there appear to be two main weaknesses. The most serious lies in a failure to distinguish between the vicarious experience of, say, a simulation exercise in a training setting and the real experience of the job – for Kolb almost any experience involving active participation seems to be a good learning experience. He has endorsed a wide range of activities as offering experiential learning, including case studies, computer simulations, the use of video, theatrical techniques, internships and even educational travel (see Lewis, 1986). Yet the thrust of the recent research and professional knowledge relating to learning for job performance which has been reviewed in this chapter implies that a necessary component of learning is the job experience itself, where transfer of learning from participation in, say, a simulation actually occurs. Supplementary experiences, though often valuable, are no substitute for the real thing.

A less serious shortcoming lies in the failure to distinguish between learning and behaviour which may or may not bring about learning. A learning style which is biased and claimed to be relatively ineffective is surely better conceived as a style of behaviour when attempting to learn which may actually block learning. The label 'learning style' tends to draw attention away from the central claim that a balanced style, or ability to draw upon a repertoire of biases according to the situation, is the most effective. According to Kolb's theory, diagnosing an individual's preferred learning style should be a precursor to developing a more balanced and effective style, rather than a celebration of human diversity. Concrete experience fanatics may, for example, learn to look before they leap.

A helpful account of how individuals' learning may be influenced by their limited awareness of their own assumptions is offered by Argyris and Schon

(1974), who developed a theory of professional learning. They suggested that individuals' assumptions constitute a theory of action governing their behaviour. A gap frequently exists between the theory of action that individuals might state to justify their behaviour – their espoused theory, and the assumptions by which others may observe them to be guided – their theory in use, of which they are largely unaware. Professionals' most common response to job related problems is to tackle them from within existing assumptions. A more effective learning strategy is to raise awareness of these assumptions, to question them and to take action in the light of this awareness. This theory highlights how individuals' actions in the workplace or in the training situation may be guided by assumptions which may be both tacit and contradict the beliefs and values they hold consciously. A rationale is offered for learning support where participants' experience is challenged by observing and offering feedback that enables them to become more aware of inconsistencies between what they think they are doing and what they are actually seen to be doing. Learning support, on this account, has a critical function in raising participants' awareness of their actual behaviour, because they have a limited grasp of their assumptions, and in helping them to improve their capacity to question these assumptions for themselves.

Schon (1983, 1987) has subsequently developed the notion of the 'reflective practitioner'. He notes how individuals display competence in the uncertain, unique and complex situations of practice, yet their awareness of how they perform their tasks so skilfully is limited. In taking action they employ knowledge that is largely tacit and intuitive. Most action is routine but when confronted by problems, they respond in one of two ways. They may stand back and reflect on their action or they may 'reflect in action', through a largely intuitive process of questioning their tacit assumptions that failed to lead to the anticipated results, and then employing other knowledge in experimenting to solve the problem. Schon suggests that initial training for professionals should include a 'practicum' in which participants tackle problematic situations. They are encouraged by a coach to think and talk as they work, so developing their capacity to reflect in action.

This development of the earlier theory directs our attention to how individuals draw upon their experience, reflect as they take action and create knowledge that is useful for practice. This process is an integral part of both task performance and learning to improve their practical competence in situations which are experienced as problematic in some way. The theory explains how Kolb's experiential learning cycle may operate, suggesting that it may take place largely at the intuitive level during concrete experience as well as cycles of action and reflection upon that action.

However, Schon does not specify in what setting the learning experience offered by a practicum should take place. If reflection in action is the basis of effective performance, surely it is important that learning how to reflect in action effectively takes place in the workplace where this performance is to be required. As with experiential learning, we must be wary of assuming that any problematic situation will do if effective reflection in action is dependent upon the tacit knowledge whose elements are, in combination, unique to each setting. Chairing a simulated senior staff meeting, for example, is not the same as being in the hot seat as a member of staff with a stake in its progress and outcomes.

All three theories help to explain the findings of the research and professional knowledge which point towards the primacy of the job experience and learning through challenge, new ideas and support in attempting to improve performance in the job. The nature of individual performance and learning for performance is explored next through an account which draws upon these theories and is consistent with the research and professional knowledge that we have explored above. Readers are invited to check their own perspective against this account, noting any points of contention. It may be helpful to consider what support for their view is provided from their own professional experience and knowledge of relevant research and theory.

A model of managerial performance and learning

The first step in developing a model of learning is to clarify the nature of managerial performance. As the Task Force report (DES, 1990) acknowledges, researchers and informed professionals including HMI have produced much advice on the knowledge, skills and personal qualities possessed by successful managers. However, one reason why the profusion of lists has failed to result in clear and consistent guidance is because different writers use different concepts – skills, tasks or competencies, for example, and they sometimes mean different things by the same concept. The account below rests upon a particular set of definitions.

Management was defined earlier as carrying out *tasks* other than teaching with and through other adults. Tasks therefore represent the work that has to be done to organize the school so that teaching and pupil learning may take place effectively. Table 2.2 is a list, developed by the NDC (McMahon and Bolam, 1990b), of the main groups of school management tasks. They consist of substantive tasks (within task areas 1–8) and process tasks (areas 9 and 10) connected with change and development.

Many management tasks involve influencing colleagues through face to face interaction, so negotiating with colleagues over the shape of the curriculum will be used as an example of a management task.

The elements of performance

Common experience, research and informed professional opinion suggest that some people perform these tasks more effectively than others. Negotiating with a colleague may be carried out tactfully or insensitively, with greater or or lesser regard for colleagues' feelings. Achieving tasks effectively is therefore a *skilful performance*, entailing the integration of several interrelated elements. To perform this management task skilfully involves *knowledge* of various kinds –

Table 2.2:   School management: main task areas (secondary schools)

Substantive Task Areas

1. *Overall school policy and aims* Philosophy, aims and objectives of the school: school development and national curriculum plans; priorities; standards; climate and ethos; equal opportunities; strategic planning

2. *Communication, organization and decision-making structures and roles* Leadership and management style: working with governors, departments and other structures; methods of consultation; provision of information; communication between staff; use and resolution of conflict; staff, department and other meetings; decision-making; problem-solving; teamwork; administration (forms); staff handbook; marketing and publicity

3. *The curriculum, teaching methods and examinations* Devising a curriculum policy in the light of the national curriculum; curriculum implementation; development and evaluation; teaching and learning methods; subject areas; timetabling; external examinations; national testing; homework policy; cover arrangements; equal opportunities

4. *Staff and staff development* Maintaining effective relationships with teaching and non-teaching staff of both sexes; staff appointments; incentive posts and allowances; job descriptions and specifications; pastoral care of staff; motivation; staff and management development: needs analysis, appraisal and provision of support, counselling and advice; delegation; role of staff with responsibility posts; teaching loads; probationers; student teachers; coping with stress; falling rolls; employment relations and unions; equal opportunities; INSET policy and programme related to LEA Grant for Education Support and Training budget and five closure days

5. *Pupils and pupil learning* Arrangements for grouping, testing and assessment; pastoral care; record-keeping; profiles; reports; discipline; regulations; continuity of education; gender, race and special needs; social and personal development for all

6. *Finance and material resources* Local management of schools budget; Grant for Education Support and Training Scheme and other budgets; buildings, equipment, furniture, materials; assessing needs; health and safety

7. *External relations* Working with governors, LEA advisers, officers and elected members; relating to parents and wider school community; involvement of parents and governors in school; inter-school liaison; links with commerce and industry; media; support services; school and the law

8. *Monitoring and evaluation of effectiveness* Roles and procedures (e.g. working parties); methods (e.g. GRIDS); performance indicators (e.g. attainment test scores, intake data, etc.)

Process Task Areas

9. *Change and development* Policy, programmes, climate, methods of review; organization development, introducing and implementing innovations (e.g. national curriculum, LMS)

10. *Self-development* Self-evaluation; personal leadership style; management of time; interpersonal skills; networks; associations; courses; exploring values

knowledge of educational aims and curriculum, and knowledge of people and the way they tend to behave. This knowledge is at various levels of abstraction and uncertainty. Recognizing the colleagues with whom managers are negotiating is relatively direct and straightforward. Some factual information, such as an account of the cost of a piece of equipment, is unlikely to be contested.

However, much knowledge (including factual information) comprises concepts or ideas through which experience is interpreted. There is not a one to one correspondence between reality outside ourselves and our interpretation of it. Managers' benign perception of their action in offering advice may be interpreted by a colleague as unwarranted interference, transgressing their rightful autonomy in the classroom. People may differ radically in their *belief* in, say, the importance of active participation by pupils in their learning or the right of managers to initiate negotiation about the curriculum. Beliefs rest upon *values*, whose source varies from simple preference to a moral principle. For example, approaching colleagues when they are busy teaching is widely regarded as not merely incorrect or foolish, but unjustifiable. Management is a moral activity involving each person's rights and responsibilities in respect of others.

Influencing colleagues to change their behaviour involves the *power* to persuade, perhaps by referring to the authority vested in the management post. Managerial knowledge therefore includes reference to the means by which each person may achieve his or her ends. Perceptions may differ about the legitimacy of each party to use certain means, depending on individuals' beliefs and values. Performing management tasks engages the *feelings or emotions* of those involved, which influence their *attitude* towards their actions. Feelings of anxiety, confidence, warmth, hostility or threat may arise prior to or during negotiation about the curriculum, for instance.

Finally, *skills* are required to perform management tasks. Skills are defined by Argyris and Schon (1974) as 'dimensions of the ability to behave effectively in situations of action'. At one extreme are simple motor skills involving physical movements, like gesticulating. At the other are complex skills involving mental operations, like the ability during negotiation to present an argument, listen carefully, pick up clues from another person's body language, and respond by defending the argument. People are viewed as possessing a skill even when they are not actually using it, so a skill refers to the potential or ability to act effectively. However, managerial skills are not knowledge-free 'bolt on' techniques that may be applied without reference to their context. Skills and knowledge are inextricably intertwined in performance of tasks. Applying a generic skill such as negotiating entails acting appropriately within a specific situation for which some contextual knowledge must be acquired. Although many contexts are very similar they are likely to differ significantly at the level of detail. Negotiating within a simulation of a meeting between colleagues will therefore differ in small but significant ways from negotiating in school.

It is common experience that people possess skills yet have limited understanding of how they use them – they cannot preach what they practice. To present an argument effectively it is essential to have knowledge about, say, the curriculum, but it is not necessary to possess knowledge which is an explanation of how negotiating works. For example, effective negotiators need not know how the brain functions or be aware of psychological theories of negotiating behaviour. We must conclude that it is unnecessary to possess knowledge explaining how a skill is performed in order to perform it. Therefore, awareness of research and professional knowledge explaining how people operate within organizations is not essential in order to perform management tasks effectively.

Conversely, it is not unknown for people to be highly articulate about how to carry out a management task while being incompetent in doing it – they cannot practice what they preach. Those who can talk but who cannot do are unable to integrate what they can explain about performance into the performance itself.

Combining elements in a skilful performance

The concept of *know-how* offers a key to understanding how knowledge and skill are integrated in performance of tasks. In his account of class teaching Oakeshott (1962, 1967) pointed to the importance of practical knowledge or know-how in skilful performance. He argued that knowing how to select and apply information requires judgement, which is revealed in action and cannot be expressed fully in words. Knowing how to apply advice about, say, waiting for a favourable moment before approaching colleagues to discuss the curriculum requires additional judgement in identifying when such a moment has arrived and how to make the approach. As the theories of Argyris and Schon suggested, we have limited awareness of the considerations which inform the judgements we make in action.

While some of the considerations that go into making judgements may be expressed in words, Polanyi suggested that we cannot be aware of them all while taking action (Polanyi and Prosch, 1975). In performing the task of negotiation people are focally aware of what is before their mind, in this case the argument they are trying to put forward. They may have subsidiary awareness of tacit knowledge including the significance of their body language, their memory of past encounters or the importance of demonstrating that they are a good listener. If they try to retain focal awareness of these considerations they are unable to concentrate upon the argument – too much analysis produces paralysis. It appears impossible for people to concentrate upon too many considerations at once. While it may be possible for managers to increase their level of awareness of their assumptions and to reflect in action in the way Schon suggests, there appear to be strict limits upon how far subsidiary considerations may be addressed in the heat of the moment. Focusing upon each one implies pushing the others into the background.

On the other hand, recent research on decision-making implies that many considerations are tackled subconsciously through *intuition,* whereby judgements are made and conclusions are drawn very rapidly and impressionistically during action to solve problems:

First, experts often arrive at problem diagnoses and solutions rapidly and intuitively without being able to report how they attained the result. Second, this ability is best explained by postulating a recognition and retrieval process that employs a large number – generally tens of thousands or even hundreds of thousands – of chunks or patterns stored in long term memory.

When the problems to be solved are more than trivial, the recognition processes have to be organized in a coherent way and they must be supplied with reasoning capabilities that allow inferences to be drawn from the information retrieved, and numerous chunks of information to be combined. Hence intuition is not a process that operates independently of analysis; rather, the two processes are essential complementary components of effective decision-making systems. When the expert is solving a difficult problem or making a complex decision, much conscious deliberation may be involved. But each conscious step may itself constitute a considerable leap, with a whole sequence of automated productions building the bridge from the premises to the conclusions. Hence the expert appears to take giant intuitive steps in reasoning, as compared with the tiny steps of the novice.

(Simon, 1989, pp. 32–3)

While it is possible to have a greater or lesser degree of awareness of the considerations taken into account in action, it seems that most of those that are intuitively taken into account must remain tacit while performing a task. Even when reflecting beforehand or afterwards, only a few of the multiplicity of possible tacit considerations may be raised to consciousness at any time. There is more to skilful performance than meets the eye.

Many management tasks are especially complex because they entail interaction between adults. Their completion depends upon the perceptions of each party, which may not be congruent, and upon the actions of both. The effectiveness of one person's action is assessed in terms of the actions of others, giving rise to the possibility that there may be unintended consequences for which managers must be on the alert. Otherwise, an unintended consequence, say a colleague's feeling of resentment that has not been made explicit, may form the background of future action guided by feelings generated in the previous encounter. Schon uses the term 'over-learning' to describe how awareness of important factors becomes lost as they are relegated to a realm of tacit and unquestioned assumptions. Initial sensitivity to colleagues' feelings may disappear as negotiation becomes a habit with repeated experience of similar (but never identical) situations. Often it is not until people's expectations fail to be met that they are given pause to reflect upon these assumptions.

Managerial performance as a problem solving process

The complexity of many management tasks renders their achievement problematic. In a discussion of curriculum development, Reid (1978) identified the features of what he called 'uncertain practical problems', which management tasks appear to share:

- uncertain practical problems entail questions that have to be answered. (Negotiation has to take place if curriculum practice is to change.);
- the grounds upon which decisions must be made are uncertain. (Managers must weigh up whether to initiate negotiation or to wait for colleagues to ask for advice.);
- the existing state of affairs must be taken into account. (Managers must accept colleagues' views and experiences as the starting point for negotiation.);
- each problem is to some extent unique, occurring in a specific time and context whose details we can never fully describe. (The mix of personalities and past history in school of those who are party to negotiation will be in some degree peculiar to the situation at hand.);
- answering questions compels us to find a path among contradictory goals and values. (Managers' views about the curriculum may be incompatible with colleagues' desire to decide what they teach.);
- it is impossible to predict precisely the outcome of the solution which is chosen or to know what the outcome would have been if a different choice had been made. (Since the effectiveness of managers' attempt to negotiate depends upon the response of colleagues, the outcome is, within limits, unpredictable. Once a course of action is taken it is impossible to go back as perceptions will have been coloured by the consequences of the action.);
- the grounds on which the decision is made to solve a problem are based upon the desirability of action as a means to an end, not an end in itself. (Managers' actions are directed primarily towards the education of pupils rather than the personal interests of colleagues, although the two may coincide.)

Viewing management tasks as entailing uncertain practical problems enables us to focus upon their skilful performance as a problem raising and problem solving process. The very uncertainty necessitates raising tacit assumptions to focal awareness and questioning what superficially appears to be happening in order not to become blind to assumptions born of repeated experience. Nevertheless, it is important not to exaggerate the degree of uncertainty; managers may still draw upon their wealth of tacit knowledge in judging how to take effective action in the light of understanding gained through the awareness raising process. Skilful performance of management tasks thus rests upon the integration of knowledge and skill through know-how which is acquired by doing the job. Since there is a strong possibility of unintended consequences, effective performance requires a questioning and reflective stance, retaining some awareness of tacit considerations on which action is based.

Learning the capability for skilful performance

Since know-how is not factual knowledge, it cannot be learned through words any more than we can learn to drive a car just by reading a book. Although what we can say may guide action, it is essential that any advice or principles are put into practice. Managers learn to negotiate effectively with colleagues by negotiating with them in the job – perhaps making mistakes and, hopefully, attempting to learn from them. The factual information embodied in a new skilful performance cannot be learned first, followed by learning the necessary judgement through action. The facts do not make sense unless they are related to direct experience of real situations. Would anyone argue that people may become competent teachers without stepping inside a school? Students training to be teachers rely initially upon their first-hand experience as pupils and later upon their practical experience in school as beginning teachers. Similarly, newly appointed headteachers and senior staff may draw upon their past experience of participating in the management of schools and their wider experience of interaction in other areas of everyday life.

No amount of reading, watching videos or taking part in role play exercises will supply the necessary experience of performing management tasks in the job situation. Transfer of learning for a practical activity like school management requires acquisition or modification of contextual knowledge and know-how. This account implies that preparatory support for carrying out new tasks and roles will have limited impact upon performance because further learning has still to take place in the new job situation. It also highlights the importance noted in the Task Force report of induction support for staff undertaking tasks and roles which are significantly new to them. To the extent that there is any overlap between the new tasks and those at which they are already competent, they will rely at first upon the know-how that they have learned previously. However, the new context requires that they modify their performance in the new situation as they pick up know-how and the necessary, often considerable, amount of new information involved.

It is important neither to overstress nor understress the uniqueness of the many contexts that managers experience in their professional and personal lives. The combination of the many aspects which make up a management situation may be unique in the experience of particular individuals. However, many elements will probably be very similar to situations that the managers have met before. In learning to perform tasks skilfully in the new situation they draw upon what they have learned from past experience and apply it to the situation in hand on the recognition that this situation shares many elements with past experience. This process is very largely tacit, occurring at a subconscious level. The amount of learning required will depend upon how radically different the present context is compared to situations managers have experienced before. Negotiating with the same colleagues day after day becomes a routine performance. At the other extreme we may consider newly promoted headteachers during the first term of their first headship, with an unfamiliar role carrying a new level of status, in an unfamiliar school, negotiating with colleagues with whom they are only beginning to become acquainted. In this case there is a considerable amount of new information to be acquired along with the know-how entailed in judging which negotiating behaviours will be effective in this new context.

Oakeshott referred to knowing how to act appropriately in particular circumstances as the 'idiom of an activity' which may only gradually be acquired through experience in the relevant circumstances. If we acknowledge that learning must include experience in the context for which a skilful performance is intended to be used, Kolb's experiential learning cycle may valuably be used to summarize the learning process for skilful performance of management tasks. Concrete experience in situations presenting uncertain practical problems may give rise to unintended consequences. These consequences may be grasped by reflection on action, using concepts as tools for thinking. Conceptualization helps learners to generalize and prepares them for the solution of other problems similar in some respects yet unique in their details. The overview thus gained guides the development of an experimental strategy for subsequent action whereby know-how is learned in the new concrete situation. While there is some flexibility for individuals to act according to preferred learning styles, this flexibility is limited by the necessity for reflective practice in the context of use.

Participants on many training courses, as we have seen, are given support with reflection and generalization but not with experimental action in the job. It is in this way that the learning process they offer tends to be incomplete, as the evidence of Joyce and Showers confirms. Experimental action within an off the job exercise (such as a simulation), perhaps with feedback, is a valuable component of learning support since it enables participants to develop judgement in integrating physical movements and mental operations within a context which is usually simpler than the job situation and where mistakes do not matter. It is still essential for participants to practice in the job what trainers may preach in order to learn the contextual knowledge and know-how in that situation.

Where participants are learning new skills, there is considerable learning required to bridge the gap between effective performance in the training setting and the more complex setting of the job. They have to learn how to adapt the behaviours entailed in performing the skill that worked in the context of training and judge when to employ them in such a way that they are effective in another context where mistakes count. Acquiring the know-how to integrate the skill into a repertoire and employ it creatively and flexibly in the job can only be learned through job performance. It is rather hit and miss whether learners will achieve the necessary learning unaided. The evidence of Joyce and Showers implies that more often than not it does not happen without support for experimental action in the job. The potential to bridge this gap exists within external training courses through the provision of activities based in schools (see Eraut, 1988) between off the job periods spent in the training setting. Some of these activities will be explored in Chapter 3.

Since people have to learn know-how for themselves, the learning process begins with each person's personal knowledge and know-how based on a partially unique experience and preferred learning style. As Knowles points out, adult learners are highly knowledgeable people, yet this knowledge originating with their experience is also limited. In learning to improve their performance they take on board new ideas in relation to the knowledge they already have, whether they modify, demolish, or simply add to their personal theory of action.

Learning support must therefore be tailored to their individual development needs but, because their awareness of these needs is limited, their wants – or perceived needs – may be supplemented by the needs that others perceive them to have. If certain course participants, for example, repeatedly trot out the same old anecdotes, they may be seen by others to have a learning need that they do not perceive: they may want to continue as the life and soul of the party, but they may also need to learn to draw learning points out of the anecdotes, or simply to listen. Since management performance is aimed at effective organization for teaching and pupil learning, individual development needs must relate to identi-fied priorities for the school as well as individual interest in improving personal performance or preparing for promotion.

For effective performance to be developed and maintained, a reflective ap-proach to practice must become a way of life, otherwise overlearning may lead to failure to notice unintended consequences. In this sense learning is never com-plete. Practice does not make perfect but thoughtful practice does make for improvement. However, reflective practice implies a positive attitude to learning in the form of a commitment to being open to surprise through reflection on the consequences of action, coupled with a readiness to act on the result of reflec-tion. Such an attitude may not be easy to develop. An easier life can be found by relying upon tacit knowledge and avoiding the uncertainty and psychological threat that may be raised by questioning assumptions. Constructive critical sup-port by a sympathetic person who may be trusted offers a strategy for overcom-ing defensiveness while protecting learners from the threat posed by exposure of the limits of their competence. The peer coaching component of the training model developed by Joyce and Showers may both meet this need for emotional support and provide the services of an observer of each learner's attempt to perform new tasks in the job situation.

We have seen how much theory and associated research knowledge helps us to explain performance and is therefore not directly necessary for practice. However, theory and research have a vital part to play in facilitating the ques-tioning of practice in some depth. Critical reflection is supported by the under-standing to be gained using abstract concepts and the evidence of research. Learners may be helped to question the beliefs and values which form part of their personal knowledge. They may consider how far their practice is morally defensible and whether it is likely to be effective when compared to the findings of studies in other schools. Developing a broader perspective on practice may therefore involve academic study but its impact upon performance will remain indirect, confined to influencing the choice of tasks and strategies for achieving them.

The key stages of learning for the performance of management tasks and the sequence in which they may occur is summarized in Figure 2.2. The diagram shows how a challenge to existing performance may be followed by several possibilities. Learning may entail some or all of the intermediate stages which lie between the original challenge and improvement in job performance. Let us take the example of tasks faced by headteachers in planning and overseeing school development in the light of central government reforms. The *challenge to existing performance* may be stimulated by government announcements in the media. Heads' *awareness may increase* further as they are forced to compare their educational and managerial beliefs and values with those underpinning the reforms in thinking through how they may respond in a way that they can justify. Greater awareness may lead to the development of a *rationale for changes* to be made in heads' existing performance of tasks associated with school development. More specific, *practical ideas on how to make changes* by, for example, engaging the staff and governors in development planning may follow from the rationale for change. These ideas may lead to *practice in making changes* by guiding actions to try out development planning processes. *Improvement in job performance* may result from gradual integration of these experimental actions into heads' approach to the tasks of strategic planning and monitoring of development.

However, as we have seen, critical awareness relating to educational and managerial beliefs and values and having a rationale are not a necessary part of job performance itself. It is plausible for managers to learn to do things correctly without considering whether they are doing the right things by proceeding from a challenge to their existing performance either to the rationale for making a change or direct to practical ideas on how to go about it.

Since managerial actions and their consequences may contradict the espoused beliefs and values either of managers or of those with and through whom they achieve their tasks, it seems desirable that the performance of management tasks is both informed rather than unreflective and justified rather than perceived as merely technical. Raising awareness and justifying action, together with a rationale for change, may be necessary for making informed and justifiable judgements about changes in the performance of management tasks.

Principles of learning support

The research, professional knowledge and theory discussed in the first part of this chapter point towards a number of generalizations about good practice in learning support for job performance which are backed by the model of skilful performance and learning outlined above. Learning support is likely to be effective to the extent it reflects the following principles relating to activities and programmes and the arrangements surrounding them.

(1) Performance in the job is an essential and major component of the learning experience.

(2) Learners' existing experience should be acknowledged and opportunities provided for knowledge of their practice to be shared.

(3) Learners' experience should be challenged through the provision of opportunities to develop new insights and frameworks for guiding subsequent action in the job.

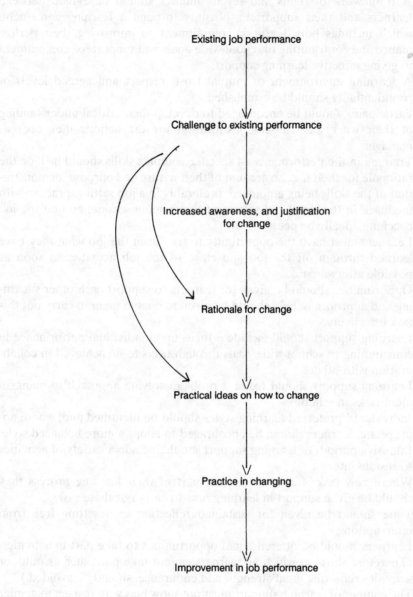

Figure 2.2:   Stages in the learning process

(4)   A framework of rights and responsibilities should be agreed between learners and their supporters, possibly through a learning agreement, which includes both learners' commitment to improving their performance and contributing to school-wide goals and supporters' commitment to giving effective learning support.

(5)   A learning environment of mutual trust, respect and agreed levels of confidentiality should be established.

(6)   Participants should be encouraged to develop their critical understanding of their work and to seek justification for the actions they take as managers.

(7)   Training in the performance of specific, complex skills should include the rationale for their use, an account of their nature and purpose, demonstration of the skills being employed, preferably in a job setting, practise with feedback in the simulated setting of the training session, and on the job coaching, ideally by peers.

(8)   Learners must have the opportunity to try out in the job what they have learned through off the job and close to the job activities as soon as possible afterwards.

(9)   Opportunities should be given for learners to support each other's learning and appropriate help should be given to enable them to carry out this task effectively.

(10) Learning support should include a focus upon individual performance in contributing to school-wide goals through tasks to be achieved in collaboration with others.

(11) Learning support should foster a problem solving approach to management tasks in school.

(12) Individuals' preferred learning styles should be identified and, where appropriate, learners should be encouraged to adopt a more balanced style.

(13) Intensive periods of learning support should include a variety of activities to sustain interest.

(14) Where new tasks for learners form part of their learning process they should be given support in learning how to carry out these tasks.

(15) Time should be given for sustained reflection in a setting free from interruptions.

(16) Learners should be offered equal opportunities to take part in activities. (Therefore those in which all learners cannot take part, such as outdoor activities requiring great strength and endurance, should be avoided.)

(17) The content of learning support must not show bias with respect to gender and race.

(18) Learning support should be given to meet management development needs identified in relation to the various purposes of continuing education, with particular attention being paid to the need for induction when starting to carry out new tasks and roles.

(19) Where there is a process of selection of participants, the criteria should be made explicit to those who are selected and those who are not.

(20) Preparatory support should be given, especially for substantial pro-grammes, which helps learners to link their current practice with the content of learning support activities.

(21) Follow-up support should be given, especially for substantial programmes, which enables learners to integrate what they have learned through ac-tivities with their normal job performance.

(22) Evaluation of learning support should include both formative assessment of the quality of the learning experience and summative assessment of the impact upon learners' job performance.

(23) Initial planning of activities and programmes should include consideration of action necessary to manage and resource all the stages from preparat-ory work to presentation of the final evaluation report.

(24) All parties with a major stake in activities and programmes should be consulted at the initial planning stage, and later stages as appropriate.

(25) Where those providing learning support, whether as facilitators or train-ers, have to carry out new tasks and roles they should be given appropriate support for their learning.

Evidently, resources will not allow all activities and programmes to follow the full range of principles. According to a considerable (although possibly inconclu-sive) body of research, professional knowledge and theory, the closer they come to reflecting these principles the more likely they are to prove effective in im-proving school management.

These principles may be used to inform the planning and management of learning support in three important ways. First, they are factors to be considered in planning and detailed design of activities and programmes. Second, they are bench marks against which to assess the quality and likely impact of learning support being offered to staff in schools. Third, they provide a source of ques-tions to be addressed by evaluation.

In the next two chapters a range of activities and programmes will be de-scribed and suggestions offered as to how they may be used in the design of programmes within the learning principles that have been established. Since new ideas are being developed all the time, the range covered is unlikely to be totally comprehensive. Activities and programmes vary widely in their complexity and there is overlap between them. Many activities described in Chapter 3 may form components of the programmes described in Chapter 4.

All the activities and programmes reflect some principles of learning support and, where appropriate, they may be adapted or used in combination to reflect additional principles. However it is important that the labels used to describe activities and programmes are not employed for modified activities which fail to reflect key principles and components that are described in the literature, other-wise confusion and even undeserved loss of reputation may be caused. For example, action learning is a well established approach in management training outside education where managers take action to solve a job related manage-ment problem (see Wallace, Bailey and Kirk, 1988). The term has been employed as a label for school management training courses where participants go no further than reviewing a management problem without necessarily taking any action to resolve it.

Readers are invited to consider which principles are or are not reflected by each activity or programme to be described and to think creatively about how the activities and programmes may be employed or adapted within learning support programmes that stand a good chance of being effective. Planning, design and evaluation issues will be discussed in detail in subsequent chapters.

3

A RANGE OF ACTIVITIES FOR LEARNING SUPPORT

Activities are arranged in alphabetical order in this chapter (for a more comprehensive source of management development activities developed outside education and associated reading see Huczynski, 1983). No attempt is made to suggest levels of difficulty since most of them may be used in various situations by people with different background experience and expertise. Certain activities refer to *processes* which are likely to be used within more substantial learning support activities. However, these processes, such as action planning or brainstorming, may also offer useful techniques for school managers to learn and employ as part of their normal job, especially when considering action and when consulting colleagues. Some activities are straightforward while others may be sensitive or more complex and therefore require preparatory work to foster the conditions necessary for success. Points to bear in mind in selecting activities will be explored in Chapter 5. At this stage it may be useful for readers to refer to Figure 3.1, which is a checklist for analysing some of the ways in which activities vary that are significant for design of learning support activities and programmes. The checklist may be used in thinking about what any activity does or does not entail.

A brief description of each activity is given, its likely impact upon job performance is estimated, and possible uses are suggested within external training courses and programmes organized by staff in schools.

Action planning

This is the process of thinking through in detail some action or sequence of actions related to job performance, both as an integral part of managers' day to day work and as part of a learning support activity or programme. One approach involves the following steps.

1. With whom do the learners learn?
   - no-one else
   - other learners
   - on their own with supporters
   - with other learners and supporters

2. What do the learners do?
   e.g. reflect
   　listen
   　talk
   　observe
   　collect information
   　practise skills
   　perform management tasks

3. What do supporters do to help learners?
   e.g. listen
   　offer advice
   　offer feedback
   　observe
   　demonstrate use of skills
   　demonstrate performance of
   　　management tasks

4. What role do supporters adopt?
   - content expert imparting knowledge and skills
   - process expert directing learning
   - facilitator for learning directed by learners

5. On whose experience, knowledge and skills do learners focus?
   - their own
   - other people's

6. On what kind of experience do learners focus?
   - school management job
   - other management job
   - experience of simulation

7. At what level of knowledge do learners focus?
   - practical knowledge related to school management tasks
   - research
   - professional knowledge
   - theory

8. Where does learning take place?
   e.g. learners' school
   　another school
   　another management setting
   　training institution

9. When does learning take place?
   - during the school day
   - evenings
   - weekend or holiday

10. On what principles or rationale does the learning experience rest?
    e.g. active participation
    　provision of equal opportunities
    　learning through job experience
    　with feedback

11. What is the likely level of impact upon participants' job performance?
    - heightened awareness
    - detailed knowledge
    - skill
    - integration into job performance

12. What support surrounds the learning experience?
    - selection process
    - preparation
    - follow-up
    - link with other activities

13. What resources are used?
    e.g. time
    　material
    　location
    　expertise
    　financial

Figure 3.1: Checklist for analysing activities

(1) Identify the purpose of the action to be taken.
(2) Consider the general strategy for action, taking into account possible risks, resources required, and implications for other areas of job performance.
(3) Specify goals within the overall purpose, with due consideration to the likelihood that goals may change as unforeseen contingencies arise.
(4) Decide when actions will be undertaken and a deadline for achieving the goals.
(5) Consider how to evaluate the action plan.
(6) Plan the first step in detail.
(7) Consider how to ensure that all necessary resources (such as time during the school day, or the support of a colleague) will be available.
(8) Consider what problems might arise and, if so, how the action plan might be modified.
(9) Decide at what point the next steps of the plan will be worked out in detail.

Action planning is an effective way of promoting focused activity in carrying out individual or shared management tasks and is thus a useful habit for all managers to learn. As a learning support activity, action planning encourages learners to follow up for themselves in their normal job what they may have learned through close to the job and off the job experiences. It is important that action planning is not viewed as a one-off event. It is most effective as an ongoing process of planning and adjustment in the light of contingencies that may arise and evaluation of what actually happens in implementing each main action step.

Action research

As the label implies, action research refers to a systematic and evaluative enquiry into a practical issue or problem coupled with action to solve it. A report may be written so that others may learn from the experience. There is a long tradition of action research conducted by teachers into their own work in the classroom (Wallace, 1987a). More recently, the approach has been adapted as a strategy for one or more individuals to investigate their own performance of management tasks (e.g. Wallace, 1986c; Day, Whitaker and Johnston, 1990). The aim is to improve job performance by raising their awareness through the investigation of a management issue connected with their management tasks, followed by planning and taking managerial action. For example, Burton (1989) gives an account of how, as a deputy head in a special school, she attempted to highlight and change attitudes to gender issues through reorganization of teaching and learning.

The process is generally viewed as a cycle or spiral (e.g. McNiff, 1988). An initial perception of an issue (such as communication problems between staff) leads to fact finding (perhaps by talking with staff or tracing what happens to circulated documents or messages). The increased level of understanding so gained informs discussion and the formulation of an action plan designed to improve the situation (say, by implementing a new system for the dissemination of written information).

The plan is implemented as part of individuals' managerial work in school and its effects are assessed (possibly by seeking staff opinions). The action is evaluated or judged through a review which leads to a new understanding of the issue and the beginning of a second cycle.

A range of methods may be used to conduct action research but, as most people in schools are unfamiliar with statistical methods and other complex research techniques, the most common approach is to go for relatively simple methods such as interviewing, observing, keeping a diary of reflections, and self monitoring while taking action (Cohen and Manion, 1989). Triangulation is a technique that is sometimes used, where the perceptions of all parties to a management situation are sought to discover if there are discrepancies and, if so, why they have arisen. Although action research may be conducted alone and without support, staff in a school may work together in collaborative action research groups, often facilitated by an outsider such as a lecturer from a higher education institution (see Lomax, 1989).

Action research is an effective way of raising awareness about performance and improving performance through taking action in the job in the light of this awareness. The approach can be rather introspective where participants rely exclusively upon their own knowledge and ways of thinking. A more powerful learning strategy may be to seek information from the distillation of experience contained in research, professional knowledge and theory in order to inform the inquiry and action in school. Some sensitivity may be required where action research is conducted into management since evaluating the consequences of managerial actions may involve investigating their influence (or lack of it) upon the actions of other adults.

Staff in a school may, individually or as a group, investigate their performance of their management tasks as an integral approach to the job. Action research may be included within external training courses as a project that participants tackle in their school between periods at the training institution. The NDC has developed distance learning modules which may be used in school (McMahon, 1991; Oldroyd and Hall, 1991b). The written report may be submitted for accreditation.

Brainstorming

This is a simple process for ensuring that, within a group, each person is able to contribute ideas about the topic under discussion and, as a problem solving technique, it enables the group to consider the fullest possible range of solutions.

The effectiveness of brainstorming rests upon all members obeying certain rules of procedure. One approach involves the following steps.

(1)	Everyone in the group is invited to contribute as many ideas on the topic or issue under consideration as they can think of, however far fetched they may appear to be. All ideas are recorded on, say, a flipchart so that the group can see them. Individuals are not allowed to evaluate other people's ideas at this stage.

(2) When initial ideas have been exhausted, individuals may ask questions of clarification about any of them and may add new ideas.

(3) If there are many ideas, some of which appear to overlap, participants who offered certain ideas agree to group them together.

(4) The relative merit of ideas is discussed. According to the outcome being sought, the group may agree to accept or reject particular ideas, or may rank them in priority order.

A refinement of brainstorming is the *nominal group technique* (Collinson and Dunlap, 1978; Fox, 1989), designed to emphasize ideas rather than their owners so as to reduce individuals' inhibitions about putting ideas forward and to prevent undue weight being given to an idea because of the status of the person who offered it. The technique works best with a group of less than ten people.

(1) Everyone is invited to write down, without reference to others, their ideas on the topic under consideration. Advance notice of the topic may be given, enabling members of the group to consult other people and write down their ideas beforehand. They bring the list of ideas to the meeting.

(2) Each person, in turn, expresses one idea which is written on a flipchart exactly as stated, and the round robin listing of ideas continues until all ideas are exhausted. A way of ensuring anonymity at the stage of contributing ideas is for individuals to write their ideas on cards which are collected in, shuffled and written up on the flipchart. This method enables several people to write up ideas simultaneously, each on a different flipchart, so reducing the bottleneck that often results from the process of hearing one idea per person during each round. At this stage no discussion is allowed and no account is taken of overlap between ideas.

(3) Individuals may request clarification of any idea on the list and only the person who offered it is allowed to respond.

(4) Repetitions are eliminated and partially overlapping ideas are combined in a more comprehensive statement where the people who contributed the ideas agree.

(5) Each person studies the amended list and ranks the ideas according to agreed criteria, such as beginning with the highest priority or the most desirable idea.

(6) Each person, in turn, calls out her or his ranking which is recorded beside the relevant idea on the flipchart. The rankings are totalled for each idea, enabling the list to be reordered according to each total score and producing a ranking reflecting the aggregate of individual views.

(7) The ranked list forms the basis for debate and decision-making.

Brainstorming and the nominal group technique are useful both as part of every-day consultation, decision-making and problem solving in schools and within learning support activities where it is intended to pool the ideas of all participants.

Case studies

A case study is an account which focuses upon some aspect of a situation, such as the introduction of a school development plan or the procedures for setting up new management structures in a school. The use of particular cases to illustrate general learning points has been widely used for many years inside and outside education (Cohen and Manion, 1989). Case studies tend to be used for two different purposes: for learners to reflect upon the experience of others whose work is reported and to consider the lessons to be learned for their practice; or for learners to raise their awareness by conducting their own investigation into management practice in their (or another) school and by writing a report.

The first purpose is encompassed by accounts of real or fictional situations where the information given is selected according to the learning focus: say, the approach to managing a school's delegated budget (e.g. Paisey, 1984; Lyons, Stenning and McQueeney, 1986; Buckley and Styan, 1988; Briault and West, 1990; Buckley, Styan and Taylor, 1990). This use of case studies is common practice in external training courses. They may form the basis of a simulation exercise or a stimulus for group discussion, and may lead to considering the implications of issues highlighted in the case for participants' action in school. Case studies which report on situations that are similar to those experienced by participants are most likely to be perceived as relevant to their job concerns.

Participants on external education or training courses may also write their own case study for the second purpose. The approach may be used for an investigation with an initially identified focus or to generate issues or problems relating to individuals' managerial work of which they were previously unaware. Methods are various, including interviewing, observation and studying documents, and participants must learn to apply them with rigour and sensitivity. Writing a case study (about, say, co-ordination between departments of a secondary school in implementing the National Curriculum) is an effective way of broadening the range of evidence upon which management decisions (perhaps to modify the range of courses offered for each year group of pupils) may be based. The materials for the Open University course EP 851 'Applied Studies in Educational Management' give a full account of this approach (see Goulding *et al.*, 1984).

Case studies help to raise awareness and, where they relate closely to learners' jobs, they may inform their management practice. The approach is especially powerful where people carry out a case study relating to their own management practice. However, case studies do not in themselves require any managerial action to be taken beyond the work of enquiry. Whatever knowledge may have been gained from the case study has yet to be integrated into improvement in job performance through managerial action in the job. Since conducting a case study effectively requires skills of investigation and synthesizing information, people may benefit from support in developing these skills (see Bell *et al.*, 1984).

Learning support activities organized by staff in schools could include discussion of the issues for the school that may be raised by reading a published case study. Alternatively one or more staff may investigate a management issue in the school and report back either verbally or in writing to their colleagues as the basis for future decisions.

Coaching

Coaching is an on the job activity which refers to the process where one person gives guidance to another so as to help improve his or her performance (Megginson and Boydell, 1979). There are two main types of coaching role. In the most widespread approach experts offer advice, demonstrate good practice, observe learners' performance and intervene to provide constructive feedback or model skilful performance. Many expert coaches have received training in the coaching process. During the last decade expert coaching has increasingly been offered to teachers by advisory teachers who work with them in their classrooms. The approach has potential for supporting staff in their management role, especially through advice, observation and feedback. More experienced staff may act as mentors for their less experienced colleagues during the period of their induction into a new management post, for example.

An alternative approach is peer coaching, advocated by Joyce and Showers (1988) as an effective way of following up training in specific teaching skills. In their model, pairs of teachers from a school who have attended the same course visit each other at work, observe, offer feedback and discuss how to perform the teaching tasks more skilfully. In contrast to the directive style of much expert coaching, peers usually operate more as facilitators since they are both learners helping each other to solve problems. Non-directive peer coaching tends broadly to follow rigorous procedures for observation of teaching known as 'clinical supervision' (Goldhammer, 1969; Acheson and Gall, 1980). The person being observed retains a high degree of control over the coaching process.

(1)   Beforehand, both partners agree upon the procedure to be followed and the focus for observation (say, how far a head of department enables members of the department to express their views during a departmental meeting).

(2)   The observer records only the information that the person being observed has agreed upon (perhaps the amount of time each person at the meeting spends speaking), rather than his or her judgements about what is observed. The record is given to the person who has been observed and a period of time is allowed for individual reflection.

(3)   The person who has been observed is encouraged through the observer's questioning to analyse the information and to judge her or his performance. The observer offers judgements on the performance of the person being observed and gives advice only when asked to do so.

(4)   The person who has been observed plans subsequent action (possibly by making a point of asking each colleague at the next departmental meeting, in turn, for their view).

Joyce and Showers argue that for peer coaching to be effective it must have a focus which is provided by the preceding joint training experience. Further, each partner should receive preparatory support as part of the training in the skilful performance of offering systematic, impartial yet sympathetic support in their coaching role. A valuable spin-off is the likelihood that staff will forge closer working relationships and develop a collaborative problem-solving stance to their work.

Peer coaching may be adapted for pairs of staff in school to give each other mutual support focusing upon specific aspects of, say, leading a secondary school department or acting as a primary school curriculum consultant. The approach may valuably form part of an external management training course where pairs of teachers from the same school attend together who have a similar level of management responsibility.

Both expert and peer coaching are very effective in helping individuals to improve their managerial performance where a supportive climate is established and the coaching has a specific task focus. Coaching is, however, quite costly in terms of time during the school day required by peers or payment for the services of an expert. It may also be perceived as threatening and care is needed to help some people to come to terms emotionally with being given constructive feedback on their performance. A combination of coaching and provision of additional relevant information through, say, lectures or reading is a particularly powerful way of improving performance while promoting a habitually reflective, problem solving approach to practice.

Consultancy

A consultant is someone who provides a service to people in organizations by offering expert advice and information or expertise as a facilitator. The aim is to help staff in schools to solve their workplace problems. In primary schools, many staff have management responsibility for an area of the curriculum in which they act both as experts and facilitators. Management consultants are widely employed by organizations outside education (Kubr, 1976). In the last few years, external consultants have increasingly been employed by LEAs and, to a lesser extent, by school staff (Gray, 1988) as changes in the funding of in-service training have enabled schools to purchase consultancy services.

Consultancy typically includes some form of review of existing management practice in a school and advice on planning how to improve it. External consultants must be skilful in collaborating with clients from other organizations in situations which may be sensitive or potentially threatening, in addition to developing and maintaining up to date knowledge of school management and facilitation techniques.

School staff may be supported in improving their work by consultants who provide a well-informed perspective on their work and encourage them to reflect, attain an overview and plan subsequent managerial action. More rarely, consultants may remain on hand to observe and evaluate the performance of staff, so providing direct support with the improvement of job performance. It is important that staff clarify at the outset what the consultant is to do and negotiate an appropriate contract or agreement.

Increasingly, school staff are engaging the consultancy services of lecturers from higher education institutions, LEA advisers, recently retired headteachers and others to support their work, for example by facilitating a strategic review conducted by the senior management team of a secondary school or by giving advice on marketing. The cost of consultancy tends to mean that a consultant's involvement with a school is for a short time, possibly spread out over a long period. Consultants frequently give inputs to external training courses. An alternative approach is described by Beck and Kelly (1989), who report how groups of participants on one management course acted as teams of consultants by investigating and advising upon an issue for staff in other schools. Preparatory support was given in learning to act as consultants.

Counselling

Counselling is closely related to coaching but the main emphasis is upon discussion and advice rather than observing and giving direct feedback on performance in the job (Reddy, 1985). People acting in a counselling role help colleagues through support which may vary from a directive to a non-judgemental 'sounding board' style. In the latter case individuals are encouraged to reflect upon their performance, job related problem or career interests, to make their own judgements, to consider ways forward and to decide upon action to be taken. Effective counselling requires the ability to listen actively and to frame appropriate questions. In co-counselling, peers in the same organization act as counsellor for each other.

Counselling may help individuals to reflect upon their practice or career concerns, to receive the emotional support to be gained from a sympathetic listener, and to plan action. It forms a major component of staff appraisal interviews. Unlike coaching, counselling generally does not include direct support during action to improve job performance. Co-counselling may form part of a school-based approach or be incorporated into external management courses.

Critical friendship

This term refers to an arrangement between two or more staff from the same or different schools who agree to provide confidential mutual support by commenting on each other's job performance (e.g. Mountford, 1988). They may discuss issues, carry out an interview or observe and give feedback on practice. Informal arrangements may, for example, be made for mutual observation during a meeting of staff with feedback afterwards. Curriculum consultants in primary schools or secondary school heads of year may pair up and agree to comment upon each other's work with colleagues. Participants on management courses may be encouraged to team up and give informal support after the course is over.

Critical friendship may promote reflection on performance and planning of action while at the same time providing emotional support.

Critical incident analysis

A critical incident may be defined as an event involving people in an organization which has given rise to problems with the achievement of management tasks (such as an unexpected demand upon the LMS budget or an acrimonious meeting). Analysis of critical incidents may help to raise awareness of the causes of problems and provide a stimulus for planning changes in management practice (Lacey and Licht, 1980). Individuals may keep a critical incident diary where they note down brief details of each incident, what led up to it, how they responded, and how they might improve the way they dealt with similar incidents in future. Analysis may be conducted by individuals or groups, whether as an exercise organized by schools or as part of an external training course. Critical incident analysis may be employed within an education course as an empirical basis for scrutiny, employing theoretical frameworks such as micropolitics.

In one group approach to analysis each member, in turn, recounts an incident. *Symptoms*, or causes that appear on the surface, are distinguished from deeper, *underlying causes* (for example, conflict between staff over the allocation of capitation within LMS may be a symptom of different beliefs and values about the relative importance of various areas of the curriculum). The group brainstorms all possible causes and likely ones are selected and discussed. As many possible solutions are brainstormed without evaluation. Solutions are then evaluated and the individual who recalled the incident decides upon an action plan.

Group memory

This is a very simple technique for use during day to day management meetings in school and within learning support activities. It is easy to lose sight of what has been said during a discussion. In some meetings or group activities it may be worthwhile to record the points made by each participant so that the issues raised and points made can be resurrected and retained for later reference. A popular method of recording is to use a flipchart. Either one person records for the group or individuals write up their own points. Usually a short phrase containing the key words is enough to trigger memories afterwards. As each sheet of the chart is filled it is torn off and pinned up so that a cumulative record is on view to the group throughout the session.

Job enrichment

This is an on the job learning support activity that may be offered in any school as part of the deployment of staff (see Wallace, 1985). A management job in school may be revised in order to include unfamiliar tasks that offer a learning opportunity to the person doing the job. The initial step is to identify the management tasks that the present job includes, possibly through reference to a job description. The next step is to consider what the person needs to learn in order to develop (for example, to gain experience of tasks that will prepare the person for possible promotion, to offer a new challenge to someone who has been doing the present job for some years and feels the need for refreshment, or to provide an opportunity to build competence in existing tasks that the person finds difficult). Job enrichment may consist of additional tasks at the present level of responsibility (say, a primary school curriculum consultant for science takes on extra responsibility for technology or a secondary school deputy chairs a working party on promoting equal opportunities for pupils and staff). Alternatively, new tasks may be taken on at a new level of responsibility (as when a secondary school teacher takes over the ordering of stock from the head of department).

This approach to on the job learning is likely to be most effective if it is planned as a learning experience and support is given by a colleague who acts as a mentor and gives counselling or coaching support. A job enrichment experience may be planned by staff within schools or linked with participation in an external training course. For example, each participant may take on new tasks prior to a course and share experience of critical incidents with others. New tasks at a more senior level of responsibility may be designed as an experience to follow up a course aimed at career development.

Job rotation

In a rotation scheme planned as an on the job learning experience two or more staff spend a period in each other's job, whether in the same or a different workplace. Often the group taking part undertakes a number of jobs at the same level of responsibility, as a way of broadening experience. Group members in the scheme may pair up as critical friends, offering each other informal counselling. In many secondary schools, deputy heads rotate administrative, curriculum and pastoral roles over a period of years. Similarly, primary school curriculum consultants may rotate areas of curriculum responsibility.

A further possibility is for staff to be seconded between schools for a restricted period, with prior agreement about the tasks to be undertaken so that each person may return to his or her post with minimum disruption. (For an account of an exchange between senior teachers with responsibility for the induction of new staff in two secondary schools see Smith and Phipson, 1982.) Each person may work on particular tasks under the guidance of a colleague in the school where she or he is working temporarily. It may be easiest to arrange a swop between schools for staff with responsibility at the middle management level.

Job rotation is also a very cost effective way of providing staff who wish to prepare for promotion with the opportunity to try out in practice, however temporarily, a post carrying more senior management responsibility. This opportunity may be presented when the more senior member of staff plans to be absent from school, perhaps when attending an external training course. A more junior member of staff may 'act up' by taking over the senior person's job while he or she is away (see West, 1987). As the person in the acting role will be taking full responsibility for the senior post it is crucial that the experience is planned thoroughly beforehand. The person may keep a journal and discuss critical incidents with the senior manager on a regular basis, perhaps over the telephone. Counselling support may be offered when the senior manager returns, to promote critical reflection on the experience. It is possible to plan, as part of an external course, provision of support for the person acting up from the manager who is attending the course. While deputy heads normally act as headteacher when the head is absent from school, usually for a short period, the learning potential of the experience may be enhanced if it is organized between head and deputy as an on the job development activity.

Learning contract

A learning contract or agreement is a statement negotiated between learners and those acting in a learning support role (Stuart, 1978). It may record what the learner will attempt to learn, how and when the attempt will be made, how it will be evaluated and whether opportunities will be available to renegotiate the contract. Where individuals take responsibility for their own development, they may make a contract with themselves to help sustain their commitment. Each person within a learning support programme may negotiate an individual learning contract, whether the programme is an external training course or one organized within schools. Equally, joint learning contracts may be made where individuals are learning as a group. Contracts imply rights and responsibilities:

● learners have responsibility for taking the learning activities seriously, undertaking the tasks involved, attempting to improve their job performance and, where appropriate, supporting other learners;
● learners have a right to conscientious, well planned and sensitive help from those in a learning support role;
● supporters are responsible for helping the learners;
● supporters have a right to expect learners to participate fully and try to make the most of the learning opportunities presented.

Learning contracts can be an effective way of ensuring clarity amongst all parties about the aim of a learning support activity and of gaining mutual commitment and effort. They foster unity of purpose for on the job learning opportunities planned in schools, possibly forming one outcome of appraisal to identify individual development needs. Learning contracts or agreements are particularly helpful with external training courses because of the gap that professional experience suggests may otherwise exist between the intentions of trainers and the understanding and commitment of learners.

Learning styles analysis

Managers are supported in identifying their habitual or preferred way of behaving when learning (see the discussion of learning styles in Chapter 2). The aim is to learn how to learn more effectively so as to exploit the wide variety of planned and unplanned learning opportunities that occur in the job and during learning support activities. The exercise of learning styles analysis raises individuals' awareness of how they operate. It encourages them to consider the effectiveness of their style and to plan ways of developing one that is more effective. Thus learning styles analysis is a needs identification procedure and individuals have to transfer what they have learned by modifying their approach to learning, whether within a training course or in developing a problem solving approach to their everyday work in school. Learning styles analysis is based upon Kolb's (1984) research and theoretical work on experiential learning. Two well known methods for identifying learning styles are Kolb's (1976) learning styles inventory and Honey and Mumford's (1982, 1983) questionnaire.

After completing the analysis, individuals plan how to supplement their preferred approach to learning by attending to parts of Kolb's learning cycle where they appear to be weak (for example, one person may tend to jump into action without pausing to reflect upon possible alternative strategies or their possible consequences; others may feel uncomfortable with experimental action unless they have had plenty of time to analyse the learning situation in depth, drawing upon their professional knowledge of similar situations).

Learning styles analysis may be employed by individuals or groups in school or incorporated into external training courses.

Lecture and discussion

Inputs by individuals with knowledge to impart are a very widespread component of learning support, often coupled with response to questions from participants and linked with discussion in plenary session or in groups. Their purpose is generally to explore ideas, to give information and to help participants relate them to their experience, concerns, and way of perceiving. Techniques to capture and hold participants' attention and to supplement what is said with audio visual aids and handouts are well known but perhaps not as widely practised as they should be. Many of these techniques are very obvious and comparatively simple to put in place (see Griffin and Cashin, 1989), including as appropriate:

● ensuring that messages are received by speaking clearly, providing simple overhead projector transparencies that can be read at a distance, or avoiding standing between audio visual aids and the audience;
● planning a lecture so that the content is presented in a logical sequence and summarizing the main points at the end of an input;

- distributing clearly presented handouts beforehand so as to save participants from being distracted by having to take full notes;
- keeping discussion groups small enough for each member to have the opportunity to contribute;
- ensuring that discussion groups have a clear brief and, if possible, a well briefed facilitator;
- restricting the content of reporting back from groups to a few succinct messages;
- employing activities for structuring group discussions such as brainstorming or the nominal group technique (see earlier in this chapter) which guard against the possibility that certain participants may dominate the debate.

Lectures are an efficient way of putting over ideas and information to a large number of people and may be both stimulating and enjoyable. Discussion, whether in plenary session or in groups, encourages individuals to explore their understanding and to link new ideas or information to their existing knowledge and way of thinking. However, while learning through these activities may inform action in the job situation it does not address the process of integrating what is learned into a skilful performance in the job.

Whether in the setting of a programme organized by school staff or an external training course, lectures and opportunities for discussion may be used to explore ideas and information. They may be supplemented by other activities such as skills training which cover other aspects of the process of learning to improve job performance.

Mutual support group

This term may refer to a variety of arrangements for peer support (Bailey, 1987). Between two and about ten staff, whether from the same or a different school, offer each other confidential help through a range of means, ranging from informal discussions to visiting each other at work. Some groups have included managers from industry and commerce. Groups frequently meet away from the job, where they may share concerns, give an input on a management issue of mutual concern, and give each other feedback and advice. An external consultant may be employed to provide a structure for the mutual support process. The consultant may help participants to organize meetings and school visits or offer preparatory support in impartial observation and feedback.

One variant popular in North America is based on principals' centres (Wallace, 1987b) which operate like teachers' centres in this country but are intended exclusively for principals (headteachers). Principals may organize their own mutual support activities located at the principals' centre, such as conferences, meetings with an external speaker, or discussion and reflective writing groups.

Mutual support groups may be effective in enabling peers to receive help from other managers who are likely to be familiar with the kind of problems they face.

Most do not provide direct support with on the job learning. Groups may be organized within a school amongst staff with a similar level of management responsibility or be linked with an external training course. One approach is for mutual support groups to be formed during a course with the intention that they will continue after the course is over. Experience suggests that they are most effective where a clear agenda is set for each meeting and they are allowed to disband once participants feel they are no longer needed. Mutual support groups have affinities with coaching and co-counselling activities but tend to have less specific purposes and procedures.

Networking

Networks within education have been defined as 'a type of voluntary collaboration between professional colleagues with a common theme or purpose' (Hall, 1988). They are a means of providing informal opportunities for communication and support between individuals with similar interests, and between people with a problem and those who may help to solve it. Individuals take advantage of the network entirely at their own discretion.

Initially a number of contacts is often made, and an arrangement is set up to facilitate others joining the network if they wish. Some means is devised whereby individuals may inform themselves about others' interests, experience or expertise. Networks may include files of contacts and other resources and some have a telephone 'hotline' through which people may be put in touch by a network co-ordinator, perhaps based in a teachers' centre. In the United States one network for principals has produced 'yellow pages' directories of principals who are willing to offer advice from their own experience with particular management problems (Barnett *et al*, 1984a, 1984b).

Networking is a potent way of of enabling school managers to give and receive advice on each other's job related problems. Most school staff develop their own network of colleagues in their own and other schools. However, their range of contacts is likely to be more limited than a network where a central person develops contacts and a system for putting people in touch with each other, and for this work some financial resource is required.

Virtually any group of people may set up a network. For example, head-teachers or deputies in the same area may agree to provide advice by telephone, or the participants on an external training course may decide to continue net-working after the course is over. For such a network to operate successfully it is important to clarify its purpose and the ground rules for contacting others to seek their support.

Personal journal

Managers maintain a daily or weekly record of significant personal experiences and reflections related to their performance in the job (Bailey, 1987). The aim is for individuals to help themselves to make sense of this experience, to plan action to improve their performance and to retain a record of key incidents in their professional lives as a basis for occasional review of their learning (see Pedler, Burgoyne and Boydell, 1978). One approach is to use the journal as a form of therapy at the end of each day by jotting down, as they come to mind, the problems faced, the solutions attempted and the managers' feelings about stressful incidents. A more specifically task related strategy is to note criticial incidents (see the description earlier in this chapter). Alternatively, for a short period of no more than a week, a brief record is made at intervals through the day of the main activities and the time spent on them. One method is for managers to write down before each day's work begins what they plan to do. They then compare these plans with the record of what actually took place.

Journal entries provide a valuable source of job based material for reflection which may be carried out alone or with the support or a colleague. It is likely that most may be learned from a journal if the content is focused upon particular issues, themes or incidents, if enough time is spent to record key experiences in depth and if sufficient time is laid aside for reflection, analysis and planning. Managers may keep a journal for a time to support their own development in the job, or as part of their activity within a mutual support group. Journals may be used within external training courses to provide a stimulus for exchange of job related experiences among participants, either as a preparatory activity before the course begins, or during a modular course between periods at the training institution.

Private study

Individuals conduct a study on their own, usually away from the workplace. They may choose the topic and the pace of learning, or may engage in work which is assessed and accredited through a higher education institution. There is an enormous range of print and audio visual material on aspects of school management which may stimulate reflection. Private study may serve the purpose of professional education, deepening individuals' understanding of the wider context of their work. It may link more closely to job performance if the focus of study arises from the identification of individual needs and a main aim is to inform the present or future performance of management tasks. Private study can prove difficult to sustain without the structure and support of some kind of programme. The expansion of distance and open learning programmes in recent years offers individuals an increasing range of topics, materials and support linked to their job as managers in school (see Chapter 4).

Quality circles

The quality circles approach has been pioneered in Japan where groups of employees, usually operatives rather than managers, become more involved in their work by solving their own job related problems with the support of managers. A quality circle typically consists of between four and ten volunteers drawn from one working group or department and their supervisor or manager, who acts as the facilitator. The quality circle meets for an hour each week in paid time. Problems are identified by members of the circle rather than by senior management and are connected with their own work, not that of other groups in the organization. Identified problems and their suggested solutions are presented to senior management for decisions about whether to implement the solutions offered. All members of a quality circle are given preparatory training in systematic problem solving and collaborating in a task oriented group (Robson, 1984).

Quality circles have been tried out in some colleges of further education (FEU, 1989). In one college four quality circles were created with volunteers from the library, administrative, technical and teaching staff. All participants received preparatory training. A co-ordinating committee supported the quality circles initiative, monitoring progress and organizing training. Problems considered included the external appearance of the college, the operation of certain courses for students, and overdue library books. Solutions were presented to college management for decision-making. One quality circle met every two weeks where the participants:

- identified a problem (for example, lack of storage space);
- brainstormed and defined causes;
- constructed a cause and effect diagram;
- arranged to collect relevant information;
- analysed information to identify the major cause of the problem;
- presented a range of solutions to management.

It appears that quality circles may be most appropriate for secondary schools and larger primary schools. A voluntary group with representation from teaching and non-teaching staff may be set up with a member of staff with middle management responsibility as a facilitator. Quality circles may be a valuable way of bringing together teaching and non-teaching staff to consider issues affecting the management of the school.

Self development

Self development is a broad concept with two main dimensions: development by the self as a process, and development of the self as a goal. Management self development activities are usually based on a combination of both dimensions. Individuals voluntarily engage in and control the learning process. They focus upon the development of their skills in, say, interpersonal relationships (Boydell and Pedler, 1978). Self development activities tend to be based upon the assumptions that learners have a positive attitude towards learning and know how to direct their own development. A range of self development packs has been produced outside education (e.g. Woodcock and Francis, 1979; Francis and Woodcock, 1982; Local Government Training Board, 1984). Typically they consist of a means of identifying personal development needs or blocks to effective managerial performance, such as a questionnaire, followed by a series of close to the job activities which can be completed alone or with one or more colleagues. Exercises include, for example, practical ways of discovering how a person uses time at work which lead to strategies for improving effectiveness in the use of time.

The NDC has produced a modular self development programme for staff with middle management responsibility in secondary schools which includes both readings and a variety of activities encouraging managers to reflect upon their job performance and to consider action to improve it (Hall and Oldroyd, 1990). The programme may be tackled in a variety of ways. Individuals may work at their own pace, a group of staff in the same school may work together, and the modules may be studied with tutorial support leading to accreditation.

Self development is mainly a close to the job activity which is effective for managers who have the capability to direct their own learning. Learners may raise their awareness of their performance through the activities and may be supported in deepening their understanding through the provision of material drawing upon research, professional knowledge and theory. They are encouraged to support themselves in taking experimental action to improve their practice as managers. The approach can offer an inexpensive way for individuals to meet their development needs. Self development activities may be organized by school staff or form a component of an external training course.

Shadowing

One person arranges to follow and observe another for a time while he or she goes about his or her normal job. Shadowing is often a one-way learning process, where a person sees at first hand how an experienced manager operates (Taylor, 1977). This form of shadowing is a refinement of the unplanned experience most managers have during their career when working with colleagues who have greater expertise. Shadowing a more senior member of staff in school may be employed as a preparatory or induction experience for, say, aspiring or newly appointed deputy headteachers. Another version, usually as part of an external training course, is for a school manager to shadow a manager from outside education in order to compare how tasks are carried out in a very different setting.

A two-way learning process is offered when the person shadowing offers feedback on what has been observed to the manager being shadowed. This process of mutual learning may occur when two or more staff from the same or different schools arrange to shadow each other and give feedback on their observations. (For a research based programme entailing mutual shadowing and feedback see peer-assisted leadership in Chapter 4.)

Shadowing is similar to coaching (see earlier in this chapter) and may follow a similar process except that the focus lies upon general performance rather than learning to use new skills in the performance of specific tasks. This activity may be an effective way to provide the observer with a demonstration of good practice and help the observed to become more aware of how he or she performs in the job. Both observer and observed have still to transfer what they have learned by taking action in their job in the light of their new level of awareness. The normal work of each person who is shadowing may have to be covered. The approach is likely to be most effective when there is an agreed focus for observation. Participants who are new to shadowing may benefit from guidance on how to observe unobtrusively and systematically and, where appropriate, on how to give and receive impartial and constructive feedback.

Simulation

Some aspect of the real world is reproduced in a simplified, controlled and sometimes highly condensed fashion (Taylor and Walford, 1978). Participants are exposed to an experience which is designed to highlight some of the problems of the real situation. They may have to make managerial decisions on the information supplied or engage in *role play* and so be protected from exposing their normal reactions. Simulations were among the first participative methods to be employed in external school management training courses.

They vary widely in the tasks that participants are set and how closely the context relates to the job setting. For example, there are *in-tray exercises*, where a participant is presented with, say, a series of letters, memos and other documents that are imagined to have arrived on a headteacher's desk. A group may build a tower out of toy bricks to learn how each member behaves in a situation where teamwork is required. At the other extreme are complex *management games* involving, perhaps, a fictional secondary school where strategic planning decisions lead to various consequences at a later stage in the game. Events and decisions that in reality take place over months or years can be addressed in a matter of a few hours.

Simulations may both help to raise awareness of issues with some link to job performance and provide opportunities in a simplified setting where mistakes do not matter to practise skills such as decision-making or chairing meetings. Participation is often an intense and sometimes emotional experience. Since, by definition, the simulation experience is a simplification of what might happen in the real job, simulations give little support for participants in transferring into the job what they have learned through the simulation. This gap may be particularly great where the simulation tasks and setting are remote from those of the job. Further, some participants may be unwilling to engage fully in the learning experience on offer where they do not perceive how a task such as building a tower relates to their job in school. Simulations may be most effective if complemented by activities that link more directly with job performance.

There is wide scope for the use of various forms of simulation in both development work organized within schools and external training courses.

Skills Training

Skills training refers to practice of a particular area of behaviour, usually with feedback on performance, which takes place in a setting away from the job. Management skills that individuals need to develop further are identified, then practised in a safe environment where mistakes may be made and feedback accepted without embarrassment (see Joyce and Showers, 1988). As discussed in Chapter 2, skills are the capacity to perform actions which may vary widely in their complexity and the balance of physical movements and mental operations they entail. Skills expressed in the performance of management tasks include negotiating, active listening, being assertive, decision-making, avoiding anxiety in a potentially stressful situation, report writing, book keeping, reviewing and interviewing.

Skills are always performed in a specific context and the actions involved in, say, being assertive, must be modified according to the context in which they are used. Therefore, while off the job skills training can prepare participants for performance in the job, they must learn how to modify their actions to use the skill appropriately in performing their management tasks in school. For example, the assertive skill of repeatedly asking for what a person wants in the face of opposition – but without being aggressive – may be taught in the training session through the following sequence of activities:

- Individuals may be offered some guiding principles or a description of a sequence of behaviour to adopt.
- They may observe a demonstration of the skill being performed effectively by the trainer in a role play exercise with a participant or through a video of the skill being used in a school setting.
- They then practise the skill in turn by performing a role play exercise in trios with one person acting as observer who gives feedback to the person practising the skill. It is essential that each person in the trio has an opportunity to practise being assertive and receives feedback.
- Once they are able to perform the skill in the context of the role play they are ready to continue the learning process by trying out and modifying the performance of the skill within their normal job.

In much skills training it tends to be assumed that participants will transfer the learning they have gained from the training into skilful performance of their management tasks in the job. According to the research discussed in Chapter 2 subsequent on the job coaching is very helpful in supporting this additional learning through provision of feedback and suggestions about how to adapt the skill as an integral part of job performance (see earlier in this chapter).

Skills training may be offered within a workshop organized by school staff or an external training course. It is common practice to employ an expert trainer or consultant to conduct the training. It is important that the trainer is able to provide a demonstration of good practice and to create a mutually supportive learning environment to minimize the threat that may be posed to some individuals.

Stress management

Stress management implies that staff develop the ability to monitor their behaviour and their emotional responses in the job, to modify this behaviour and to employ a variety of strategies designed to reduce feelings of anxiety and pressure. Stress arises from a combination of pressures related to the achievement of management and other job related tasks, individual physical and mental reactions to pressure, and the coping strategies that people use to reduce or control stress (Dunham, 1984). A rough definition of stress is reaction to job pressures which is greater than individuals' coping resources, resulting in poor job performance.

The first step in stress management is for individuals to identify and accept that they are showing symptoms of stress. The second step is to select strategies which may focus upon one or more factors: reducing pressures relating to job tasks (say, by delegating more tasks to colleagues), and improving coping strategies (perhaps by developing a regular relaxation routine). The intention is to improve job performance by changing individual physical and mental reactions to situations which induce stress and, where possible, by avoiding such situations.

There is a range of activities for identifying and managing stress. Individuals may take on self development activities related to the job, such as analysing how they spend their time in school, or less directly related activities like relaxation skills training, meditation or developing a hobby. Activities involving colleagues include examining job descriptions to achieve a more equitable workload, developing a critical friendship between, say, a head and deputy for mutual observation and feedback, or counselling where, perhaps, a headteacher has a wide ranging and confidential discussion with a colleague who is showing symptoms of stress (see earlier in this chapter). These activities may be organized by staff in a school or form part of an external training course. Since stress management entails the skilful adjustment of job performance it is important that activities go beyond the identification stage to learning support with reducing and controlling stress.

Team building

In most organizations, including schools, effective management implies coordinating the achievement of management tasks which, in turn, implies collaboration between several people. The aim of team building activities is to develop a group of managers, each of whose work is affected by the others, into an effective team with commitment to mutual support and maximizing individual contributions. It is assumed that a group of managers working collaboratively as a team is more effective than individuals working on their own (Woodcock, 1979).

However, teamwork may not be necessary for many routine management tasks (Critchley and Casey, 1984). The first step in considering the need for learning support through team building activities is to decide whether teamwork is required for effective performance of the task. Critchley and Casey argue that intense teamwork is necessary mainly where there is shared uncertainty about joint tasks. The incremental way in which central government's educational reforms are being introduced in this country has resulted in a high degree of shared uncertainty about the tasks involved in planning and implementing multiple innovations alongside ongoing work. Arguably a team approach is needed for strategic planning, monitoring and adjustment of action to orchestrate these changes.

The process of building teams may take considerable time and may be approached in a variety of ways. Many activities are designed to diagnose blockages and directions for individual and group development. Off the job or close to the job activities include games designed to reveal the need for mutual trust (see development and outdoor training in the next chapter), simulations entailing a joint task which no individual can achieve on her or his own, and analysis of each member's preferred roles within a team, coupled with the attempt to agree upon complementary roles – for example, one person chairing meetings while another ensures that tasks are completed (see Belbin, 1981). On the job activities may include the analysis by an observer, perhaps an external consultant, of each member's behaviour during the conduct of a meeting of the team (see Rackham and Morgan, 1977) and giving feedback afterwards on, for instance, who interrupted others or who spoke the most.

Diagnostic team building activities may help members to raise their awareness of individual needs, behavioural styles and the blocks to effective performance of the whole team. Team members often endeavour to improve their individual and group performance without further external support by, for example, rotating the chairing of meetings. One alternative is to engage the services of a consultant over a period to give guidance, observe and give feedback to the team.

Team building work may be carried out with any group with joint tasks that cannot be achieved effectively without the commitment of each member and without co-ordinating his or her contribution. It is suitable for senior management, pastoral, department or faculty teams in secondary schools, and for the whole staff of primary schools. A popular activity at the beginning of many external training courses is team building among participants, usually from different schools, to foster mutual sharing and learning support throughout the course. What such activities cannot do is influence directly the strength of teamwork in school except where participants from the same school attend the course.

Visits

One or more school managers visit a different workplace, either another school, an educational establishment such as the LEA offices or a non-educational establishment (for example a factory, a bank or a hospital). A common aim of visits is to observe management practice in another setting. The visit may include various activities, such as a tour of the site, a meeting with managers, observing a meeting in progress or shadowing a manager at work for a short period (see earlier in this chapter). Visits may be designed as a one way or a two way learning experience. Intervisitation schemes may entail reciprocal visits to each party's workplace on one or more occasions.

Visits may be an effective way of raising awareness about how others fulfil particular management tasks and in stimulating reflection upon managers' approach to their own work. The more similar the workplace being visited is to the visitors' setting, the easier it is to perceive links with their own practice. On the other hand the more different the setting, the greater the challenge to visitors' habitual ways of perceiving how management tasks are performed and the greater may be the intrinsic interest of experiencing a different work environment. Visits can provide little learning support with transferring what has been learned into improvement in visitors' own job performance but they may be complemented by other activities such as action planning and peer coaching. In order for individuals to be released during the school day, it is necessary to provide some form of cover.

One or two way visits between participants' schools or one way visits to non-educational establishments may be organized by school staff or form part of an external training course. Intervisitation arrangements are often used to promote close liaison between neighbouring schools of different phases.

Visits may have a broad or narrow focus. In the former case, visitors sometimes have difficulty in deciding what may be significant for their own management performance. It is therefore important that visits have a clearly understood purpose and structure. They are potentially disruptive to ongoing work in the place being visited. It is likely to be worth considering ways of minimizing such an impact, for example by negotiating a suitable time, agreeing the number of visitors, consulting those whose work will be observed and reaching prior agreement about levels of confidentiality.

4

A RANGE OF LEARNING SUPPORT PROGRAMMES

Many learning support initiatives have been designed as a programme of activities which link together to provide a comprehensive experience. In this chapter several major types of programme will be discussed. As some are complex and sophisticated while others are relatively simple, certain programmes will be explored more fully than others. Readers may find it helpful to consider what combination of activities is offered in each programme (including the activities outlined in the previous chapter); how far the programmes are consistent with the principles established in Chapter 2; and how these programmes may be used, possibly with some adaptation, in their own situation. The checklist for analysing activities (Figure 3.1) may also be applied to programmes, bearing in mind that a programme may consist of a number of activities.

Action centred leadership

This term refers to a view of leadership developed by John Adair (1979, 1984), drawing on his experience outside education. Where a task must be achieved by a group, leadership should be adaptable to match the constantly changing situation. For a group to be successful three types of need must be met. *Task* needs cover the necessity of achieving the task; *group* needs refer to the degree of collaboration between group members that is required; and *individual* needs are a reflection of personal drives, which include the need for self-esteem, for acknowledgement, for acceptance by the group, or for achievement. Adair argues that leaders must ensure that all three types of need are met as far as is possible.

This approach to leadership is learned through short, off the job action centred leadership courses, consisting of brief inputs followed by group exercises designed to highlight the key leadership concepts. A set of tasks is given, such as building a tower out of toy bricks, watching a film which displays aspects of leadership behaviour and their consequences, or a role-play activity. Feedback is provided on members' performance in meeting the three types of need, how far they have been able to communicate effectively, and on the problem solving strategies adopted. Participants plan action in the workplace that they intend to take in the light of what they have learned. In recent years some courses have been offered to headteachers.

Action centred leadership courses provide opportunities for participants to raise their awareness of their behaviour in a group situation, to analyse it using a simple set of concepts and to try out strategies to improve their leadership performance in that setting. However, like other kinds of programme that take place off the job these courses appear to give little support with experimental action in the job itself. Participants are often drawn from different organizations and so may not represent a workplace team, and the tasks are mainly a form of team building simulation. Greater benefit may be gained if action centred leadership courses are linked with follow-up support in the job setting.

A more powerful learning opportunity may be offered where the courses are offered to working teams within one organization. It may be possible for a large school to arrange for, say, the senior management team to attend such a course and to follow it up with other team building and co-counselling activities (see Chapter 3).

Action learning

More than thirty years ago Reg Revans, dissatisfied with traditional off the job education and training for managers in industry, turned this form of learning support on its head by developing an approach based upon a combination of on the job or close to the job activities, together with off the job mutual support. Revans believes that managers learn most effectively with and from each other by solving real organizational problems and reflecting on their experience (see Revans, 1972, 1982). Revans's ideas have been elaborated by his followers (e.g. Pedler, 1983; Mumford, 1984; Kable, 1989) who have developed a number of variants on the original experiments in action learning. The approach is widely used outside education and is beginning to be employed in school management training (Wallace, Bailey and Kirk, 1988).

Problems are defined as complex, open-ended issues or concerns requiring action, where no solution currently exists and the solutions suggested by skilled and reasonable people are likely to differ. Revans emphasizes that the greatest potential for learning lies in solving significant *problems* as opposed to mere puzzles. The latter are defined as issues or concerns for which a solution already exists although it may be hard to find. An example of a school management problem is how to modify existing procedures for strategic planning in order to cope more effectively with central government, LEA and other innovations while minimizing the extra workload for staff that participation in strategic planning entails. An associated puzzle might be to decides upon dates for strategic planning meetings when all those required to be there are able to attend.

The rationale for tackling real problems has much in common with the model of managerial performance and learning put forward in Chapter 2. It is argued that managers work in a situation of some uncertainty where effective performance entails both responding to and initiating change in a way which is appropriate to the situation. Since the environment is not wholly predictable managers must learn to act in dealing with changing circumstances by developing their ability to question, analyse and take initiatives. They need to learn both technical knowledge, which can be taught through conventional courses, and the ability to ask discriminating questions so as to cope with the ambiguity to which new problems and new situations give rise. The latter ability may be learned by tackling actual management problems in such a way that managers are obliged to ask discerning questions, seek solutions and put them into practice. In other words, for effective learning it is essential to take managerial action to solve problems; analysis of a problem and recommendations for action are not enough to improve job performance. Moreover, managers are perceived as more likely to be motivated to learn when dealing with issues of immediate practical relevance and importance to them than when being required to reflect upon general theoretical issues or artificial problems presented through case studies or simulations.

The principle of tackling real problems is applied through the *project*, consisting of a problematic task to be achieved within a particular setting. Each person may work on a different project or contribute as a member of a group working together on a single project. Certain criteria are critical for the selection of projects:

- the nature and scope of the problem to be addressed must lie within the manager's authority to act. This authority may already exist or be given when the project is selected;
- the problem must be open-ended yet feasible to solve in the medium term (say, within six months);
- it must relate to an identified priority for improving the organization through a management task or set of tasks;
- senior managers in the organization must be prepared to back the participant in taking managerial action.

It is possible for the project task and its organizational setting to be familiar or unfamiliar to a particular participant (see Table 4.1). Suppose a participant is the experienced headteacher of a secondary school. A project to solve a familiar task in a familiar setting (Box 1) might be to improve the procedures for communication in the school. If this same head undertook the same project when newly appointed to another school it would constitute a familiar task in an unfamiliar setting (Box 2). An unfamiliar task in a familiar setting (Box 3) during the early 1990s might be to develop an approach to strategic planning that takes into account innovations such as school development planning and the budgeting cycle within LMS. Finally, an unfamiliar task in an unfamiliar setting (Box 4) might be for the secondary head to devise a new approach to strategic planning for a neighbouring primary school.

Table 4.1: Range of action learning tasks and settings

		Task Familiar		Unfamiliar
Setting	Familiar	1		3
	Unfamiliar	2		4

Projects in an unfamiliar setting (Boxes 2 and 4) were often undertaken in the early days of action learning on the grounds that the potential for learning is greatest in a situation where managers have to learn plenty of technical knowledge before they can begin to ask sensible questions and take action appropriate in the context. However, more recently the focus has shifted towards tasks in a familiar setting (Boxes 1 and 3) where participants may focus upon the learning associated with analysis and managerial action without having to spend time acquiring contextual knowledge that may be of little direct use in the future. Further, it is argued that the project will be of more immediate interest as it relates more closely to solving problems in their normal work. As we saw in Chapter 2, the more divorced a learning support activity is from the job situation, the more new learning is required to transfer what has been learned through the activity into improvement in job performance. A project in an unfamiliar setting may be an unnecessary luxury extra when there are plenty of management problems to solve in school.

Two support roles for participants, usually fulfilled by different people, are commonly identified in action learning programmes outside the education sector. The *sponsor* is responsible in some way for a participant's development as a manager, and may be the person to whom the participant is accountable or a management development specialist in the organization. Sponsors are involved in the identification of participants' needs in relation to their normal job or in preparation for possible promotion, and in choosing an action learning programme as an appropriate way to meet these needs. During the programme sponsors obtain feedback from the participants about their progress and any difficulties they may have, such as conflict with the demands of the rest of their work. The *client* is the person who initially identifies the problem to which the individual or group project is directed, enables the participant to gain access to information and support from staff whose work relates to the problem, and backs the participant when he or she is implementing action to solve it.

In the education sector the roles of sponsor and client are often combined. The Task Force report urges that headteachers take responsibility for the development of their staff. Therefore, headteachers appear to be the sponsors of senior staff who take part in action learning programmes. Since heads are responsible for the day to day work of the school within policies agreed by the governing body, they are most likely to be the clients who have 'ownership' of problems connected with participants' job in school. Where heads join action learning programmes the sponsor may be the LEA within its legal responsibility for professional development of staff in schools, and heads will most probably act as their own clients in identifying a problem connected with their work that they wish to tackle. Headteachers are likely to have the authority necessary to explore a management problem in their school and to implement a solution to it. Where their staff take part in action learning and work on a project based in the school, it is crucial that headteachers give full support to their work as senior staff may otherwise not have the authority needed to implement a solution to the problem. Senior staff should therefore consult headteachers regularly as their project progresses.

The rationale for managers learning with and from each other rests upon a view of learning as a social process of mutual self help. Other managers know what it is like to be confronted with intractable problems and therefore will have some empathy with a manager's situation. Managers are in a good position to promote each other's learning by asking critical questions as they may often bring relevant experience to bear. A neutral situation with sympathetic peers is held to be more conducive to the frank offer and receipt of constructive criticism than the workplace where managers are less likely to be willing to admit that they have problems.

The principle of managers learning with and from each other is applied through the action learning *set*: regular meetings of groups of four to six managers with a facilitator known as the *set adviser*. The latter acts as a process consultant, helping the group to work together effectively and ensuring that participants devote some time to reflection on their learning and consideration of their personal development as well as focusing on their projects. Casey (1983) suggests that the facilitation role of the set adviser includes helping participants to:

- offer support through penetrative but constructive questioning of the person reporting on her or his project, rather than satisfying the questioner's personal concerns;
- develop a positive attitude towards receiving and actively seeking support from other members of the set;
- comprehend the components of action learning and how to implement the project solution within each participant's organizational context (by, for example, negotiating about the problem to be solved and the recommended solution with the senior managers who will be affected);
- facilitate their own learning as a group.

It is essential that set advisers are centrally concerned for participants' learning and avoid imposing their own views when, say, participants do not appear to perceive a solution that the set adviser thinks they should.

A common pattern of set meetings is monthly over a six to nine month period. The meetings must take place in a comfortable setting where members will not be disturbed. Set meetings provide opportunities for:

(1) a regular process of reviewing members' project work, exchanging ideas and information, and action planning;
(2) peer group pressure upon members to sustain their individual work;
(3) inputs and advice relevant to the projects given by experts drawn from outside the set;
(4) insights about tackling management problems, about themselves as people, about their feelings when taking risks and experiencing stress, and about how they learn as individuals and as a group;
(5) mutual encouragement when individuals are experiencing difficulty.

Sets may consist of managers from similar or different settings. Bailey (1987) reports on the value of a mixed set, containing headteachers and advisers, in providing a wide range of perspectives on problems which promotes the questioning of habitual assumptions.

In the last few years action learning has begun to make a significant impact upon external management training courses for schools. These courses are often based upon a series of modules or blocks of one or more days spent in the training institution, during which time the sets meet, interspersed with several weeks in school when participants work on their projects (for further detail of one approach see the account of a course of this kind at the end of Chapter 7).

Monitoring by the NDC suggests that action learning has generally been very well received by participants. In cases where some of the principles and procedures have not been followed (by, for example, organizing sets without a set adviser or participants going no further during the course than planning managerial action to solve the problem) there is evidence that some of the learning potential may have been lost (Wallace, 1990a). While the principles and procedures of action learning allow much scope for diversity of training practice it does seem important that programmes are designed within the parameters set by these principles and procedures.

Another initiative has been to incorporate action learning as one component of accredited courses for managers from outside and, more recently, inside education. These courses are often at Master's degree level (e.g. Pike, 1983; Thorpe, 1988; IMC, 1988). Generally, the action learning component is assessed on the basis of what participants write about their project, as opposed to how they perform as managers. Some courses take assessment closer to performance by asking senior managers in participants' organizations to corroborate their account of the project. Senior managers give their view of the effectiveness of participants' performance in solving the management problem which formed the focus of the project.

Projects undertaken in unfamiliar settings are valuable learning experiences in themselves but are no substitute for the real thing: learning in the job situation. Action learning appears to have greatest potential for the improvement of job performance where projects focus upon management problems in participants' work as school managers. Opportunities are provided for reflection, with the aid of other managers, and participants are expected to take experimental action in the job. However, support for actual job performance is generally limited to help within the set for reviewing work on the project and action planning for the next few weeks' work connected with it.

It is possible that managers may unwittingly 'pool their ignorance' by operating within their existing assumptions and habitual ways of thinking. This constraint may be avoided through relevant inputs which offer new concepts and perspectives that help participants to interpret their experience and inform their plans for managerial action. Set advisers may take on this responsibility. Alternatively, additional activities within a programme may present participants with a range of theories and research evidence from which they may derive prescriptions for practice. Advanced education courses which include action learning appear to offer an appropriate structure for such an input. However, it does seem important that designers of these courses avoid a divorce between academic learning and the action learning set by providing support for participants in linking theory, research and practice over and above the opportunities they receive for discussion in the set.

It is common for sets to comprise one manager from each organization. While this arrangement may aid frank discussion in the set, participants are on their own in tackling their problem which, it has been argued above, should be based on their normal work. If two or more managers from the same part of the same organization attend, there seems a better chance that they will form a 'critical mass' in the workplace, with the possibility of giving mutual support on or close to the job in tackling their problem. Time may be arranged for them to work together in school on a shared project. Under these circumstances they are more likely to engage in the learning necessary to improve their job performance than if they are working alone. A compromise arrangement may be for colleagues in school to agree to support the participant who joins an action learning programme.

Additional issues revealed by the NDC monitoring visits are, firstly, that the ground rules for activity within sets should be established at the outset and participants expected to work within them. These ground rules may cover:

- levels of confidentiality within the set;
- whether participants are allowed to give advice or whether they may only ask questions of others to encourage them to think of solutions for themselves;
- the procedure by which each participant in turn has a limited amount of time to give an update of progress and to be asked questions. All participants then reflect on how they are learning and engage in action planning.

Secondly, set advisers who are new to this role benefit greatly from preparatory and induction support and opportunities for ongoing exchange about their problems as set advisers. An initiative taken by the NDC, which was well received by those who participated, was to form an action learning set of novice set advisers, facilitated by a very experienced set adviser. Harries (1983) suggests that preparation and induction of set advisers may valuably include:

- inputs from experienced set advisers;
- watching a video of a set in action;
- experiencing a set as a participant;
- working with an experienced set adviser in the role of co-adviser to a set.

Thirdly, except where participants are headteachers, it is crucial to gain their headteachers' support for their project and to consult them before implementing solutions, especially where the problem tackled may lead to changes which affect the management of the school. There have been instances where heads have been dismayed at the solutions proposed to problems of which they have no sense of ownership. Finally, it is beneficial if the focus of action learning sets includes raising participants' awareness of how they are learning. Mumford (1984) suggests that individual learning styles should be considered and participants encouraged to modify them where necessary for a balance between engaging intuitively in immediate experience, reflective observation, abstract analysis and experimental action.

As we have seen, considerable interest is being shown in action learning within the sphere of school management and it has been incorporated in several external education and training courses. The approach could be adapted for use in programmes organized within schools, perhaps for several middle and senior managers within one secondary school or for deputies in neighbouring primary schools. (For a useful practical guide to planning an action learning programme see Pearce, 1983.)

Development and outdoor training

In development training for managers participants usually work in small groups to achieve various joint tasks, sometimes in competition with other teams. Many programmes designed for managers are based out of doors (Bank, 1985) and may involve strenuous physical activity. One definition of this form of learning support is a 'strategy which through the integrated use of the outdoors and process reviews, seeks to develop the effectiveness of individual and group performance in the work setting' (Beeby and Rathborn, 1983). This approach has diverse origins, including adventure training for young people where the emphasis is upon personal development through challenging experiences, and army training using outdoor simulation exercises for teams of soldiers.

In management development the team tasks are viewed as a vehicle for encouraging members to reflect upon their individual and collective performance as leaders and followers. A key component of development training programmes is the *process review* which follows each activity and is intended to highlight the learning that is taking place. Typically members of each team are briefed by a facilitator; they tackle their task while the facilitator observes their interaction and their approach to solving the problem with which they are faced; and they then take part in a process review.

The facilitator invites participants to explore their feelings during the activity and to consider which actions contributed towards or hindered the achievement of their task. While participants may be primarily concerned about the substantive task, the facilitator focuses their reflection upon themselves as learners. According to Beeby and Rathborn, trainers and facilitators should have the expertise to offer a range of theoretical inputs from time to time in response to participants' evolving needs; to sustain the momentum of a sequence of action and review cycles; to modify planned programme components as issues emerge from participants' response to the tasks; and to model good practice in the process of giving and receiving feedback. In addition, it seems evident that they require sensitivity in supporting participants who may be emotionally distraught, the capacity to encourage them to reflect on their behaviour and, where potentially dangerous physical activities are involved, expertise in guiding novices safely as they engage in the activities.

Some programmes are jointly facilitated by expert trainers and managers from the client organizations who help participants reflect upon the implications of their experience for their job performance. Where groups consist of people who work as a team in their job, they may be encouraged to explore how their behaviour in the training setting reflects issues connected with their performance as a team in their everyday work.

Tasks vary enormously, their impact often depending upon the element of surprise – participants usually do not know what they will be required to do until the briefing. Examples include being given a limited array of materials from which the team must build a raft and cross a river within a specified time; some team members being blindfolded and having to trust others to lead them around and over obstacles, whether indoors or out; each team improvising a short play which is performed to other teams; finding a way of moving a heavy object over a certain distance without it touching the ground; or solving a series of clues and searching for a hidden object. Some tasks can be quite complex, occupying a day or more, including outdoor sports such as canoeing and climbing in a simulation where each team has to amass points by achieving a series of tasks.

Development training is often designed to provide a very intense teamwork experience, heightened by the intellectual and emotional impact of unfamiliar tasks in an unfamiliar setting. Where participants are strangers to each other the experience is in some ways even more dramatic as they have to learn very quickly to accept, trust and collaborate with people they have never met before. Thus development training is deliberately intended to place participants in a situation which is radically different from their job. Issues connected with teamwork and personal behaviour are raised in a much shorter space of time than would normally occur in the workplace. For this reason development training for managers is commonly designed as a residential programme of several days situated at a specialist centre isolated from the outside world.

Development training for managers, whether outdoors or not, is essentially a form of simulation, modelling aspects of job situations and providing participants with extensive feedback on their performance in the training context. They may be given repeated opportunities to reflect upon their behaviour, possibly using concepts offered through various inputs, and given support in planning and implementing experimental action. Beeby and Rathborn argue that development training accords with Kolb's theory of experiential learning (discussed in Chapter 2), each component of the programme providing support for a particular stage of the learning cycle (see Table 4.2).

Table 4.2: Application of Kolb's theory of experiential learning to course design

Kolb stage	Course component	Function
Concrete experience	Indoor and outdoor exercises	Generation of learning data
Reflection/ observation	Process reviews	Identification of emergent issues
Abstract conceptualization	Theory	Clarification of experience, insight
Active experimentation	Planning	Preparation for action on the course and at work

(Beeby and Rathborn, 1983)

Since Kolb does not distinguish between the experience of a simulation and the experience that the simulation is supposed to model, Beeby and Rathborn appear to be correct. The evidence presented in Chapter 2 suggests that the simulated experience – however powerful – in a situation which is explicitly designed to be in many ways divorced from the job context, is not sufficient in itself to meet their stated aim of improving job performance. Little support is offered, beyond help with action planning towards the end of the programme, to enable participants to transfer their learning to the radically different job situation. As the NDC monitoring visits revealed, where colleagues from the workplace have not shared the Damascus Road experience of development training, they may not find an individual's change in behaviour acceptable. Where working teams are trained together their shared experience may form the basis of subsequent mutual support in the job. It seems probable that, whether participants are from different organizations or are working teams, complementary follow-up support in the workplace will help them come down to earth and gradually integrate their learning into improvement in job performance.

The strong risk element designed into development training, often both emotional and physical, implies that specialist expertise is needed for trainers and facilitators. Therefore it seems sensible that, whether development training forms part of a programme of activities organized within schools or an external training course, people with this expertise are employed to carry out the training – it is not a job for amateurs!

Education courses

Long, external award bearing courses typically have a modular structure and may be studied on a full or part-time basis. Some institutions providing education courses, such as the University of Bristol, are increasing their accessibility by including distance learning modules alongside those taught within the university, and schemes have been devised to enable individuals to transfer credit from one institution to another for modules satisfactorily completed.

Many in-service courses at first degree, diploma or higher degree levels include a management component and a number of diploma and higher degree courses are devoted entirely to management. Most courses include some form of project which may link more or less closely to each participant's job, and study for a degree by research may be based on an investigation into some aspect of school management practice. The skills developed for a study of this kind may relate indirectly to some of the skills required by managers: for example, the ability to analyse, create new ideas, and write a precise, logically argued report. Study of the theoretical bases of management practice raises awareness of the complexity and dilemmas of school management, giving participants the conceptual tools to analyse their work in school.

Education courses, whether studied at the host institution or at a distance, are an immensely significant form of learning support. They are the sole type of support for school managers which focus centrally upon deepening their understanding of the social and political context in which their school work is set, helping them to clarify and justify their educational and managerial values, and introducing them to a range of concepts and research knowledge that may be used critically to analyse their practice. It was argued earlier that effective management performance includes the ability to make informed judgements about which educational and managerial values to pursue in addition to the skilful performance of management tasks themselves. Education courses may offer the necessary intellectual grounding for making informed judgements.

This depth of understanding may be combined with learning support for job performance, especially where participants study on a part-time basis, through projects which encourage individuals to take experimental action in school in addition to the common practice of collecting evidence from the school for a written assignment or seminar (see action learning above). As a programme of support for management development it is important that participants are helped to connect their theoretical and research knowledge, which is an explanation of performance, to the knowledge required for performance itself.

It is possible, though not yet common practice, to plan a combined learning support experience which includes an education course alongside activities which are not part of the course itself but relate more directly to performance. For example, a manager may study an accredited distance learning course and also engage in, say, shadowing or a critical friendship in the workplace.

Fellowship

A fellowship is an opportunity for individual study, often lasting one term or more, based with an institution which provides in-service training. In addition to expert supervision given by a tutor, fellows have access to resources such as a library and contact with others who have similar interests. As a learning support activity for school managers, a fellowship generally combines personal development with an aim to improve management in the fellow's school or across the LEA. The topic for investigation is negotiated between the individual and the LEA that is commonly responsible for the secondment, in consultation with the training institution which has expertise in areas such as methods of investigation and knowledge of relevant literature (see McMahon and Bolam, 1990a).

A fellowship may be conducted by a single individual identifying, for example, management development needs arising from assessment of the National Curriculum in primary schools or from LMS in secondary schools. Several fellows may work as a team, planning and piloting major initiatives such as school development plans or an LEA appraisal scheme for schools. Fellows from different LEAs may support a regional initiative to improve provision of management development opportunities for school managers by, say, designing a major learning support programme.

Fellows may benefit from the broadening of their experience, frequently having contact with a large number of their colleagues from other schools, which deepens their understanding of aspects of their work in school. They also experience performing new tasks in a new setting. Their learning about the substantive topic may inform practice in their school when they return. However, fellowships do not generally give direct learning support for job performance as a manager in school.

It may be possible for a large school or a group of schools to support a short fellowship from devolved in-service training money and, possibly, the LMS budget, to carry out specific tasks. For example, a pyramid group or primary cluster may second one person for a month to set up a major joint staff development initiative.

Open and distance learning

Open learning implies making learning opportunities as widely accessible as possible and giving learners a high degree of control over their learning experience. Distance learning is one variant of open learning with a long pedigree in educational management where access is broadened by enabling learners to study away from the teaching institution, but where learners do not necessarily control their own learning (Binsted and Hodgson, 1984).

The rationale for both open and distance learning is, in part, to remove some of the constraints upon learners imposed by many forms of learning support. Coffey (1977) suggests that some constraints are *administrative*. They may include studying in a particular place, at specified times or over a named period and being a member of a group of a certain size. Most of these constraints can be removed by open and distance learning. Other constraints are *educational*, including a pre-specified sequence of teaching, teaching method or set of learning objectives; entrance requirements which do not relate directly to participants' learning goals; and a method of assessment that does not relate closely to the way in which participants will actually use newly acquired knowledge and skills. Much distance learning, for example accredited Open University and correspondence courses, retains educational constraints upon learning whereas open learning aims to give as much control as possible to participants over what and how they learn.

Open learning has grown rapidly in recent years with the advent of computer and video technology which allows learners considerable freedom. Computer based open learning packages for managers outside education reviewed by Binsted and Hodgson include a business game to be played on a microcomputer; an interactive video package on how to cope with an underperforming subordinate; and an in-tray exercise also designed for interactive video. Thus these packages tend to take the form of simulations, some of which provide models of good practice through short video sequences. According to Binsted and Hodgson, computer based packages vary in the degree of openness afforded to the learner in practice, whether because of the design of the material or because of the ease with which learners may gain access to the package.

Similarly, distance learning courses vary in the degree to which they rely solely upon learning at a distance. Telephone and face to face tutorial support is regarded as a key component of Open University courses for school managers (Preedy, 1988), and is offered to support the materials produced by the LEAP project sponsored by LEAs and the DES. Moreover, the materials themselves may be used in different ways. Many Open University materials may be purchased separately and studied in whatever way learners wish but without tutorial support. Similarly, the distance learning materials produced by the NDC are designed to be used on their own as an open learning resource from which learners may pick and choose; as a distance learning course with tutorial support; or as an accredited distance learning course with tutorial support and assessed written assignments (see Hall and Oldroyd, 1990; Hall and Wallace, 1991; McMahon 1991).

The design of open and distance learning material does, in general, allow considerable flexibility to learners, thereby broadening access. However, the approach offers learning support mainly for acquisition of information and deepening understanding by investigation and analysis of work related issues, facilitated where there is tutorial support. Evidence for this claim is offered by the results of an evaluation survey conducted by Open University staff on the course EP 851 where managers conduct case studies in their schools. Respondents reported:

> . . . an increased understanding of management issues; increased self-confidence personally; critical analysis of their own working procedures and leadership styles; awareness of the complexity of organizational processes; insight into the value of consultative decision-making; fostering staff awareness of the need for an in-formed basis for policy-making.

(Preedy, 1988, p. 152)

Thus the course informed action in school to improve performance but did not in itself develop specific skills.

Computer based packages support learning in a simulated setting of skills with a large component of mental operations as opposed to physical movements. Some distance learning materials encourage learners to take action in the workplace which is informed by the ideas presented, but provide no direct support. For example the NDC materials for primary school managers are designed to be used by groups in school. An option, with the support or direct involvement of the headteacher, is for the materials to be used as the stimulus for a co-ordinated effort to improve their work together in managing the school. Thus while open and distance learning are excellent for raising awareness about practice and may foster experimental action in the job they appear not to offer direct support for job performance and do not seem particularly suitable for the learning of complex interpersonal and predominantly physical skills, where practice and feedback are particularly important.

As yet there is little computer based open learning designed specifically for school management. Packages are expensive to design and some require equipment for their use to which few school staff have ready access. It is much cheaper to use open and distance learning programmes based upon print material, sometimes supplemented by audio or video tapes, than to send participants on a conventionally taught course. Following a programme outside the school day minimizes potential disruption for pupils caused by staff being out of school.

This form of support may be used in several ways according to learners' needs. Open and distance learning courses may be be used by groups as part of an initiative organized by school staff or studied by individuals for their own development, possibly with resources from the LEA. Such materials may be complemented by close to the job and on the job activities which provide direct support for action to improve performance in the job, such as shadowing or coaching.

Organization development

This is a complex form of process consultancy aimed at improving the the ability of school staff to work together effectively and to achieve job satisfaction. The focus is on changing the performance of the organization as a whole by improving the way interdependent groups work to achieve corporate goals. The approach has been widely employed outside education (e.g. Woodcock and Francis, 1981) and adapted for schools (see Dalin and Rust, 1983; Schmuck and Runkel, 1985). Activities within an organization development (OD) programme will include support for staff with management responsibility. Thus a team building exercise, for example, may be extended to all the adults who work in a school. Activities may take place in the workplace or elsewhere.

OD entails the participation of members of an organization in examining current, largely internal problems and their causes; seeking agreement upon shared goals; developing a more effective group approach to problem solving; establishing structures and procedures for achieving the agreed goals; improving the working climate; and evaluating the results of their improvement efforts (Schmuck, 1982). The consultancy includes a range of activities which focus on helping staff to:

- make internal communication more effective;
- clarify individual goals and seek ways of developing joint ownership of goals for the organization;
- uncover conflict and develop the ability to collaborate;
- improve procedures in meetings;
- use techniques to assist problem solving;
- make decisions with the commitment of staff that is necessary for implementation.

The underlying aims of these activities are, first, to develop a strong, shared professional culture where each person's role is understood and accepted by others; second, to develop the capacity of staff for collaborative problem solving through systematic diagnosis of gaps between ideals and actual practice, the active search for resources to narrow these gaps, the formation of *ad hoc* groups who can take remedial action using these resources, and occasional evaluation of diagnosis, resourcing and action.

OD may contribute to improving the processes and procedures through which staff work together in achieving the tasks of management. Staff are provided with shared opportunities to raise their awareness of their performance in relation to others in the school, given guidance in ways of improving practice and offered some on the job support for joint action to improve job performance. Thus support is offered to individuals only in so far as they have a part in joint tasks and little consideration is given to support with improving individual performance of substantive management tasks. Those who have participated in an OD consultancy have still to integrate techniques for, say, clarifying and reaching agreement about goals into their habitual way of working once the consultant has departed. It can be expensive for a school to employ an external consultant and the question arises about how far staff come to depend upon her or him to sustain the initiative to improve their ability to collaborate. (For a comprehensive assessment of organization development see Fullan, Miles and Taylor, 1980.) An account of how OD has been used in British schools is given by Lavalle and Keith (1988).

Peer-assisted leadership

This is a structured form of shadowing and coaching developed in the United States. It will be especially instructive to readers who are concerned with the design of effective learning support for school managers as both the content and methods are grounded in research. A training manual has been developed in the light of repeated trialling of the programme (Barnett, Lee and Muller, undated). Pairs of principals (headteachers) or vice principals (deputy heads) shadow each other at work and conduct reflective, non-judgemental interviews after each period of observation, using a model of instructional leadership (promoting effective teaching and learning) to focus both the shadowing and the reflective interviews (Barnett, 1987). The leadership model is based upon research into the factors that effective elementary (primary) school principals take into account when leading their schools (Dwyer, 1985). The more effective principals were found to relate their managerial actions to an over-arching perspective or vision of their school settings.

The peer-assisted leadership (PAL) programme is designed to incorporate the components of training that, as we saw in Chapter 2, the research of Joyce and Showers has shown to be associated with effective in-service training for teachers. Participants are trained in shadowing, reflective interviewing and the skills of systematic analysis through presentation, modelling, practise with feedback in the training setting and some feedback during training on shadowing that has taken place in the workplace. However, the major purpose is to employ these skills as a means to the end of mutual support with improving job performance. Participants give each other non-judgemental feedback on job performance and facilitate re-flection, understanding and the attempt to take experimental action to improve practice. In other words, they are trained in the specific skills of a form of peer coaching, which they put into practice through peer coaching which is related to the way principals operate in promoting effective teaching and learning.

While PAL is not directed towards coaching principals in specific skills con-nected with principalship, the skills of peer coaching all tie closely with aspects of job performance. For example, shadowing has links with observation of teachers in the classroom, reflective interviewing has links with appraisal interviews, and anal-ysis has links with establishing a vision for the school and for strategic planning.

In the original research the investigators, from a neutral standpoint, repeatedly shadowed principals and conducted reflective interviews where principals were asked to clarify and comment upon what had been observed. Principals reported how the experience had been valuable for them as well as for the investigators, as they had been stimulated to reflect upon their performance. The non-judgemental feedback they received had helped them to see how far their intentions matched their behaviour and whether the expected outcomes of their actions had been realized.

PAL consists of six full or half day training sessions for a group of about ten pairs of participants with the same level of managerial responsibility, spread over a year (see Figure 4.1).

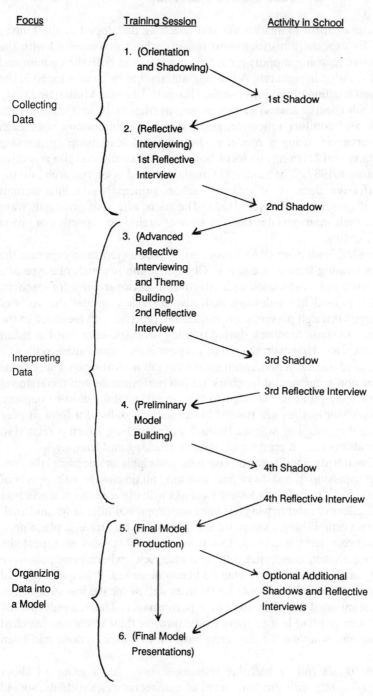

Figure 4.1:   Programme of PAL activities

In addition each participant will shadow his or her partner and be shadowed by the partner at least four times, for three or four hours on each occasion. In the first couple of training sessions participants concentrate on the skills of collecting data through shadowing and reflective interviewing, using the instructional leadership model to guide what is observed and to provide a framework for asking questions. Once they are competent in shadowing and reflective interviewing participants focus within the next two training sessions upon analysing and interpreting the data that they are continuing to collect upon their partner through shadowing and reflective interviewing. In the remaining training sessions participants are supported in developing a profile of their partner's work as an instructional leader, using the categories of the research based model as a framework. They give a short presentation to all participants which forms the basis for comparison of similarities and differences in approach. Pairs are encouraged to continue to support each other after the programme is over.

The training process for each new skill, for example shadowing, follows a similar sequence.

(1) The trainers first provide background information and suggest how it will be used in general terms.

(2) They use exemplary materials derived from the original research to demonstrate the outcomes of good practice in using the skill. For example, in the case of shadowing, the trainers present a completed set of notes made while shadowing.

(3) Participants are given opportunities to try out the skill in the training situation. In preparing for shadowing they observe a role play exercise between the trainers who act out interactions between a principal and various members of staff or parents.

(4) Participants then receive feedback from the trainers. Feedback after the shadowing role play focuses on how far participants' observation notes are focused upon areas of behaviour identified within the instructional leadership model and whether the notes are descriptive rather than evaluative. In addition, the notes made by participants during the first time they shadow their partner are sent to the trainers, who give participants feedback on the notes at the next training session.

Since participants may conduct their first reflective interview away from school, they are given preparatory training in the second training session of the kind just described. Their notes taken during their first shadowing experience are returned, with feedback, by the trainers. They then conduct the interview with their partner on the basis of these notes, with the trainers available to observe the process and give feedback. Thus the trainers offer feedback on aspects of performance of skills in the real – as opposed to simulated – situation wherever it can be made possible without them visiting the participants' schools.

Evaluation by participants both during each training session and after the programme is over suggests that PAL may influence job performance in several ways:

- participants become more reflective about their day to day activities in a way which they tend not to have found the time to do before;
- they gain insights about other ways to perform the job by observing and interviewing a partner from another school and make comparisons with their own performance;
- they find the research based framework guides their analysis of their partner's work and comes to guide their reflection on their own work;
- they pick up practical tips from each other;
- their sense of isolation is reduced and, where they find that their partner tackles aspects of the job in a similar way, they feel that their own approach is validated;
- they develop trust and respect for their partner and other participants;
- they are perceived by colleagues in school to set a good example by demonstrating their willingness to learn.

PAL appears to provide a learning support process which stimulates reflection upon performance and a means of conceptualizing and focusing these reflections. Support for experimental action to improve performance in the light of heightened awareness may be offered through subsequent cycles of shadowing and reflective interviewing.

There is great scope for this approach to be adapted, whether as a programme developed by staff within one school or a group of schools, or as part of an external training course. In the former case it is advisable to seek the support of professional trainers to facilitate the process of selecting partners; to ensure that the skills of this form of peer coaching are learned effectively; and to offer a conceptual framework which will help focus the observation and feedback cycles between partners. The PAL approach to training for peer coaching could be used to prepare the way for subsequent training in more specific skills once pairs have become competent in observing and giving feedback on performance. After perhaps two cycles of shadowing and reflective interviews pairs could receive preparatory training and observe each other in school working on, say, personal time management, drawing up the LMS budget, or interviewing parents.

Training courses and workshops

By far the most widespread form of externally provided learning support for school managers is the training course, which may last from half a day to several weeks. In addition, short workshops are increasingly a major form of support, whether planned by school staff or offered by external agencies. They are usually focused upon improving job performance and may include a wide range of activities. The impact of a course or workshop is likely to depend on the mix of activities included. We have already discussed the limitations of external courses in Chapter 2, in particular the difficulty of bridging the gap between participants' performance in school and their performance on the course. Design considerations will be discussed in the next chapter. The key to effective courses lies in the attention paid to ensuring that the course, including associated preparatory and follow-up activities, enables participants to relate their existing experience to their experience of the course and gives learning support with transferring what they have learned on the course into practice in the job.

Workshops often have more restricted aims than courses. In the short time generally available it is difficult to do more than raise participants' awareness about an aspect of performance, to give more or less specific information, to demonstrate the use of a skill and to provide practise of performing the skill in the workshop setting. Complementary activities such as peer coaching may enhance participants' ability to integrate the skill into their performance in the job.

5

MANAGING AND DESIGNING LEARNING SUPPORT PROGRAMMES

This chapter concentrates upon the *process* of designing, implementing and evaluating activities and programmes to meet identified needs. Within this process detailed consideration is given to the *content* of designs for learning support that are consistent with the principles set out at the end of Chapter 2.

At the risk of appearing to patronize readers (which is certainly not intended), it seems worthwhile warning against the possibility of alighting too hastily upon activities or programmes that at first reading look interesting or exciting. It is all too easy to come up with a design which represents a solution looking for, and soon causing, a problem. The management training field is littered with abandoned bandwagons: activities which were at one time regarded as a panacea but which participants found not to meet all their needs for learning support. All the activities and programmes described and assessed in Chapters 3 and 4 are means towards the end, however indirect, of helping school staff to learn to improve their managerial performance in the interests of better education for pupils. They vary considerably as to which aspects of the learning process they support most effectively and under what conditions. Therefore, the design of learning support must centre upon the school: the management development needs of those whose learning is to be supported should be the starting point. Only when it is decided what is to be learned and we are clear about the likely impact of different activities and programmes upon learning should we move to consider which support strategy to adopt.

On the other hand it is important to be realistic about the level of generality of the needs that particular programmes may be designed to meet. Much depends upon the feasibility of tailoring programmes to meet individual or group needs among prospective participants, which may vary at the level of detail. Arguably, under present levels of central government funding of learning support for management development in schools, most LEAs and schools simply cannot afford intensive, individualized programmes for all eligible staff in any year. Moreover, the discussion in Chapter 2 implies that by far the most significant learning opportunity lies in doing the job itself. Hence, as the Task Force report states, a major focus of learning support initiatives should be to find effective ways of helping staff to make the most of the many learning opportunities which may be found in their everyday work. As was stated at the beginning of this book, most managers eventually achieve at least a reasonable degree of competence even where their learning is unsupported.

Learning support programmes will have to be targeted upon priority areas of need. Those developed in school stand a good chance of being directed towards identified individual, group or school-wide needs. By contrast, a broad spectrum of identified needs may have to be covered by external training courses offered on a regional basis. Within such courses, the attempt should be made to provide opportunities for individuals to meet their particular configuration of needs. A crucial element is the arrangements which may be made to support the forging of a link between the course experience and their job performance in school.

One or more activities and some sets of activities designed as programmes may be incorporated into a programme developed either by LEA staff, trainers from higher education institutions or elsewhere, or by staff in schools. If the principles covering the processes surrounding learning (such as preparation and follow-up) are to be followed in addition to those encompassing the learning process itself, it is essential that even a single, relatively simple activity is planned to link closely with participants' job experience. These considerations imply that the most effective way to conceive of design is in terms of programmes which support the learning *process* rather than one-off *events*.

Designing programmes within the principles of learning support entails first deciding upon the aims of the learning experience and then considering in respect of each activity or set of activities conceived as a programme:

- which stages in the learning process it supports most effectively;
- for substantial programmes, how it may be located most effectively within a sequence of activities;
- the resources it will require, whether financial, material or human;
- the risks that it may fail to give the intended support and the safeguards which may reduce these risks.

We will examine these factors in detail when discussing the design of learning support. While they will be addressed in turn in this chapter, programme managers will probably wish to move back and forth between these factors as they begin to firm up the programme design. First, however, we will explore how designing fits into a wider management process.

Programme management

Programmes have to be made to happen and the interests of the various stakeholders in the provision of learning support must be taken into account. While the details of the management process may vary according to the scale and origin of an initiative, the main components may apply to all situations. Managing learning support for school managers implies a sequence of activities at two re-lated levels, as Figure 5.1 indicates. These activities cover not only planning and delivery but also the various components of evaluation. In this model of the management process definitions of the various components of evaluation put for-ward by Eraut, Pennycuick and Radnor (1988) have been adopted.

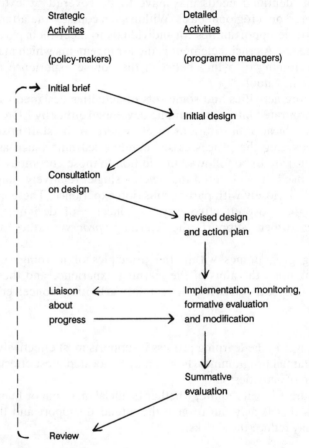

Figure 5.1: The process of programme management

Detailed activities cover the process of design, implementation and evalua-tion of programmes. Two key task areas for programme managers are the administration of a programme and detailed designing and directing. These tasks may be the responsibility of one or more individuals or of a team. For example, the programme organizer for an external programme may be an LEA adviser or lecturer in a training institution, and the director may a consultant trainer or a team of seconded headteachers. In a school both organizing and directing may be carried out by a senior member of staff responsible for staff development, or there may be a separate director, say, another teacher or an external trainer.

It was argued earlier that if programmes are to be fully effective they should not occur in a vacuum but be located within a framework of procedures at LEA and school levels for management development of school staff. Detailed activities link, therefore, with *strategic activities* entailed in liaison with policy-makers responsible for managing school management development. For a programme organized within a primary school, oversight may be the responsibility of the head, with the support of governors. A secondary school may have a staff development committee which co-ordinates internally organized programmes. There may be a steering committee for a regionally provided external programme consisting of representatives from local LEAs, from an institution which is contracting to deliver the training, from industry and from schools. Liaison between policy-makers and programme managers should take place at several points between the initial idea for a programme and the final report after a programme is completed (as Figure 5.1 implies). Close liaison is important for at least three reasons:

(1) a programme should be designed to provide learning support in order to meet priority management development needs;
(2) the detailed design, the commitment of resources, the sequencing and the timing of learning support activities will probably have to be negotiated with policy-makers;
(3) programme managers are generally accountable to policy-makers for the quality of the learning support experience they provide, its effectiveness in achieving agreed aims, and how far it represents value for money.

The programme management process will be summarized prior to exploring certain components in more detail. The first step is for policy-makers to draw up an *initial brief* in consultation with the programme managers. Whether this brief is written or not it is important to clarify the aims of the proposed programme in relation to identified high priority management development needs, the target group who will participate, and the broad parameters including a budget and a timeline within which the programme must be designed. The *initial design* is produced by the programme managers in the light of the brief and the design considerations mentioned above, commonly taking the form of a detailed and costed proposal. At this stage it seems essential that *consultation on the design* takes place between policy makers and programme managers so that the design may be revised if required before resources are committed to it. The *revised design* forms the basis for developing an *action plan* covering implementation and evaluation of the programme.

One of the secrets of success with most learning support initiatives is careful planning at the outset to ensure that all necessary arrangements are put into place in sequence. For any programme that reaches to the heart of job performance there is no guarantee that everything will go smoothly nor any certainty that the aims will be achieved. Therefore it is essential to consider how to monitor and evaluate as well as to deliver the programme itself so that adequate opportunities are taken to gather relevant information. It may also be worth considering contingency plans in case any problems should arise. *Implementation* entails various co-ordination tasks, depending upon the content and complexity of the programme, which must be carried out before, during and after each activity.

It is important to *monitor* what is happening during the programme to check whether it is going to plan and to be ready to respond to any need for immediate changes. *Formative evaluation* implies collecting evidence from participants and others involved, ideally immediately before the programme begins and at intervals while it is happening (which will depend, of course, upon the scale of the programme). Formative evaluation implies making decisions about any *modification* to the programme in the light of evidence collected. These decisions rest upon judgements about how well the programme is going in relation to its aims, the significance of any unintended consequences, and the value to be gained by possible alterations. *Liaison about progress* between programme managers and policy-makers will be advisable both to secure approval for any major proposed modifications and to ensure that those who are ultimately responsible for the programme are kept informed. *Summative evaluation* entails making judgements after a programme is finished about how far the learning support experience has been worthwhile and the value of its outcomes in respect of the programme aims. In some cases, where these aims include making an impact upon job performance, summative evaluation may have to wait for relevant evidence to be collected, say, a month or more after the programme is over. Finally, programme managers and policy-makers come together for a *review* to judge whether the aims, assumptions, activities and the overall approach to learning support should be changed.

The initial brief

An initial programme brief offers an outline within which programme managers may work. They require a clear statement of the management development needs that the programme is to meet. Needs may relate directly to the performance of present or future management tasks or to informing job performance more indirectly through deepening understanding. Once needs related more or less directly to management tasks have been stated, the purposes to be served by learning support may be clarified (as outlined in Chapter 1).

Needs and purposes, coupled with an overview of what the programme can feasibly be expected to achieve within resource and other foreseeable constraints, should inform a statement of programme aims. These aims should cover both the learning experience and the anticipated outcomes. It is a simple matter to come up with aims at a high level of generality that no-one will want to challenge. Yet if they are to be of any practical use, aims must be specific enough for programme managers to operationalize in their design and to form the basis of criteria for evaluation.

The target group to be supported varies from relatively homogeneous to highly heterogeneous in terms of job role and experience, depending on the programme. Individuals are obviously more likely to be known personally to programme managers responsible for a programme developed within a school than to those designing external programmes. For example, we may be considering all members of staff in one primary school; a mix of senior managers from schools, LEAs and industry; all heads of secondary schools in an LEA who have been recently appointed to their present post; or women teachers in the region who are interested in promotion to a post carrying substantial management responsibility. Programme managers must have knowledge of the participants whose learning support they are to plan since activities vary in the support they give and the risks they may represent to participants.

The further that broad parameters can be specified at the outset without rigidly determining the design itself, the simpler the design task becomes. Many parameters will be obvious, especially for initiatives taken by school staff. However, some of the parameters that programme managers may wish to be clear about, depending on the programme, could include:

- the total amount of time available, whether any activities may take place during the school day, any times for the programme which are fixed and any times over which there is flexibility;
- the locations for activities and their relevant facilities;
- the provisional financial budget and what kinds of expenditure it may and may not cover;
- that part of the budget which is set aside for evaluation;
- the possibility of covering staff for activities during the school day;
- the possibility of including preparatory and follow-up activities;
- the possibility of using the expertise of professional trainers and evaluators;
- the availability of people who have the ability and experience to act as facilitators or the possibility of providing preparatory and ongoing support for facilitators.

Finally, a date should be agreed for policy-makers to be consulted on the initial design.

Design considerations

Designing is a very creative task which may be tackled in diverse ways according to the preference of programme managers. The set of design steps put forward in this handbook is based upon the model of learning and the associated principles of effective learning support outlined in Chapter 2. While the nine major design steps have to be presented in turn, it is strongly recommended that they are considered together in determining a sequence of activities which makes up an initial programme design. These design steps are as follows.

(1) Consider the programme content.
(2) Consider which stages of the learning process are implied by the programme aims.
(3) Consider which aspects of the support offered by various activities promote the transition from one stage of the learning process to the next.
(4) Determine which activities may be used to supply particular aspects of learning support.
(5) Consider how far colleagues from the same school may support each other's learning through these activities.
(6) Determine the order and timing of activities.
(7) Assess the resources required to implement the activities.
(8) Consider the risks inherent in activities and ways of safeguarding against them.
(9) Consider how the programme will be monitored and evaluated.

Each of these steps will now be described in detail and strategies will be suggested that readers may find useful in setting about the design of activities and programmes.

Programme content

The first step is to consider the content of a programme, which may vary from an exclusive focus upon learners' job related concerns to a substantial input drawing upon research, professional knowledge and theory. In a general handbook of this kind, it is not plausible to set out in great detail the management topics that may be covered by the many types of programme with their very different purposes. Instead, some key sources will be mentioned briefly and we will concentrate primarily upon the process of learning and how to support it.

Hopefully, the initial brief will provide programme managers both with an idea of the management development needs of individuals or groups in relation to management tasks and with a statement of the aims of the programme. Sometimes it will be very clear what the content must be, as in the case of workshops to introduce a major external innovation like appraisal, or when prospective participants have indicated particular tasks for which they need help. For programmes less specifically linked to particular management tasks, say, an external training course for career enhancement of women teachers and those from ethnic minorities, there may be the potential for considerable choice over the ground to cover. One starting point is to consider the task areas that school management entails. Readers may wish to refer back to Table 2.2, which provides a reasonably detailed list, based on research and professional knowledge, from which programme content may be selected. In addition, for some substantial external programmes it may be possible to plan for prospective participants to review their management tasks as a preparatory exercise and to leave some time available during the programmes for support in response to the needs they identify from this diagnostic activity.

Another key source is our knowledge from research and professional experience about how school management contributes to schools that are effective in educating pupils, how we may improve the effectiveness of schools, and how we may improve the effectiveness of the management function itself. As in the case of the knowledge base about how managers learn and how to support their learning, our knowledge of effective schools, effective school management, school improvement and management development is at the same time extensive but inconclusive. Nevertheless, this work does provide some pointers about management task areas and how they may be individually and jointly fulfilled that is far better grounded in evidence than any individual's personal view could possibly be. Some programme managers may therefore wish to tap what research, professional knowledge and theory exists by checking through the relevant literature, including research reports (e.g. Rutter *et al*, 1979; Mortimore *et al.*, 1988; Louis and Miles, 1990), syntheses by academics (e.g. Bolam, 1988; Fullan, 1991), recent HMI surveys and reports (e.g. Scottish Education Department, 1989) and enquiry reports (e.g. House of Commons, 1986).

Of course some management tasks that many school managers are required to undertake by central and local government are undergoing change, as we discussed in Chapter 1. Programme managers will not have to look very far in identifying content relating to major education reforms. Where tasks change, what contributes to improvement and effectiveness may also change. In this country ten years ago, who would have considered the ability to manage a very large budget or to market a school as vital elements in contributing to school effectiveness? Therefore, another important source for the content of certain programmes is new task areas currently being implemented or on the horizon. While it may be too early to know from professional experience in the UK about how these tasks may effectively be tackled, there is frequently some knowledge which has been written up from other countries where these innovations have been tried.

Clearly, where programmes are planned to include a focus upon participants tackling management topics or problems of concern to them, whether in schools or elsewhere, this area of content will be provided by them. An issue for programme managers is how far they may intend to offer learning support that not only aids the process of investigation and, possibly managerial action, but also provides ideas and information from other sources to illuminate the topic or problem. Planning to be responsive in this way may have implications for ensuring that a wide range of resources is available, as in the case of a library, and possibly going further and expecting to plan inputs once the programme is under way. In the latter case it is essential that enough time is available to plan new inputs, especially where neither participants nor programme managers have the relevant expertise and negotiations have to be conducted with a third party who will provide some form of stimulus.

Matching learning with learning support

It is necessary to clarify how the learning process is promoted by different forms of support prior to considering the next two design steps. The model of learning for managerial job performance developed earlier (see Figure 2.2) provides a framework for analysing the components of the learning process that activities within a programme may support. There it was argued on the basis of research, professional knowledge and theory that the learning process begins with learners' existing performance; it entails some form of stimulus to change, reflecting certain beliefs and values; and results in gradual development of the capability to integrate new information and skills into skilful performance of management tasks in the job. The main components of learning support and the components of the learning process which they promote are summarized in Figure 5.2.

The left hand side of the diagram sets out the main components of the learning process. Transition between each stage and the next may be promoted by one – or for most intermediate stages two – components of learning support. These components are subdivided to highlight key dimensions in which the type of support they provide varies.

Some form of *diagnosis* helps individuals or groups to bring present behaviour into question and identify a need for change. The focus may vary widely from their *general behaviour* as adults both inside and outside work to very specific aspects of their *job performance*. This challenge to existing performance may lead to the attempt to develop awareness and to justify proposed changes according to educational and managerial beliefs and values.

The development of *critical understanding* about the job and its wider context is brought about by exploring the beliefs and values that inform learners' actions in the job. Since this process is essentially cognitive, learners may explore the perspective through which they interpret their performance – their theory of action – by drawing on a vast range of concepts and ways of interpreting practical experience. These concepts and perspectives may be more or less abstract and more or less directly linked to the job. As we discussed in Chapter 2, they inform the choice of actions and therefore are reflected in but are not a necessary component of job performance itself.

Critical understanding may be promoted by exploring concepts and perspectives from two main sources which are not completely distinct. One source is *research, professional knowledge and theory*, the stuff of educational courses and books, which constitute a distillation of practical experience interpreted through various concepts within a range of perspectives. Promoting critical understanding from this source is a powerful means of encouraging learners to question assumptions that underpin their personal theories of action. The second source is practitioners' *personal theories of action* themselves, the interpretation of their personal experience which may, of course, embody concepts and generalizations drawn from research, professional knowledge and theory, often in a relatively unrigorous way. A common limitation of reliance upon practitioners' personal theories lies in the probability that they may share unquestioned assumptions.

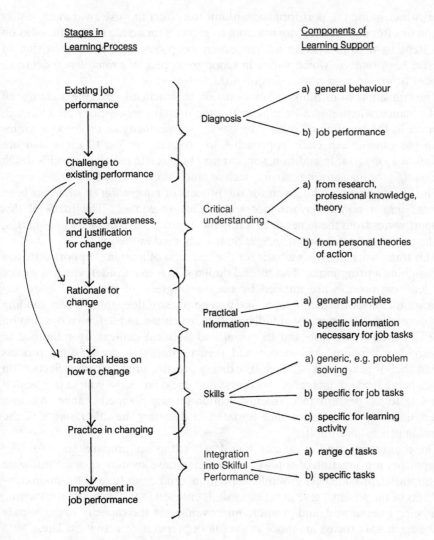

Figure 5.2:   Linking the learning process with learning support.

Increased awareness and the attempt to justify a change in performance leads to the development of a more specific rationale, usually embodying concepts within a perspective reflecting a particular set of educational and managerial beliefs and values. Equally, it is possible that a challenge to existing performance may lead directly to a rationale from within the learners' existing theory of action or provided by, say, a consultant or trainer, without a major effort to increase awareness and justify the change through development of critical understanding.

A rationale informing the change to be made links with more specific practical ideas on how to bring about this change in performance. It is plausible that a challenge to existing performance may lead directly to the provision of practical ideas which guide the performance without the effort to raise awareness, justify action or offer a rationale. Moving from a rationale for action to specific ideas on the steps to take in making a change may be promoted by the provision of *practical information* which varies in scope from *general principles* to detailed, *specific information necessary for job tasks.*

The transition from thinking about action to practice in making a change in performance, whether in a training institution or in the job, is promoted through support in the learning of *skills.* The degree of specificity of these skills varies from the *generic,* especially approaches to *problem solving,* to those that are *specific for job tasks.* In addition, support may be given in developing skills which are *specific for the learning activity,* such as study skills, for example.

Finally, support may be given for the process of *integration of what has been learned into a skilful performance* within the job context. The focus of this support varies from the general, covering the approach to a broad *range of tasks,* to the particular, referring to *specific tasks* embodied in the job.

This framework provides a basis for the selection of learning support activities in designing a programme. The second design step is to consider which stages of the learning process are implied by the aims agreed in the initial brief. An education course, for example, is likely to emphasize deepening understanding and developing the capacity of individuals to articulate and defend a position on topics related to the job and its social and political context by reference to research, professional knowledge and theory. Stages in the learning process would therefore be the challenge to existing practice arising from reflection on topics being studied, increased awareness and, in so far as the course is intended to relate to job performance, the justification for any planned change. Where a direct link with job performance is stated in the aims the other stages in the learning process are implied.

On the other hand a school based workshop to prepare staff for the compulsory introduction of appraisal may aim to raise awareness of the rationale for appraisal, provide background information, offer an outline of the main components of the scheme, give practice of skills entailed in the tasks of interviewing and being interviewed, and promote improvement in the capacity to participate in the appraisal process in school as a result of preparation activities. These aims emphasize certain stages of the learning process: the challenge to existing practice posed by the novel tasks of participating in appraisal, understanding the rationale for change and practical ideas on how the change is to be made, together with practice in changing and improvement in job performance.

The third design step is to consider which components and subcomponents of learning support to offer in order to promote transition between stages of the learning process implied by the aims. The education course may develop critical understanding both through research, professional knowledge and theory, and through the articulation of personal theories of action. Other stages of the learning process may be left for students to work through without direct support from the course.

The appraisal workshop may provide a diagnosis in terms of the central government mandate for schools to implement appraisal; offer practical information, from general principles to specific information necessary for participating in an interview; and, within the setting of the workshop, give opportunities to practise the specific skills of appraisal interviewing. Participants may be left to transfer this learning into job performance for themselves.

` There will be some differences in the stages of learning implied by programmes with different aims. In the example of the education course, all seven stages are implicit where the aim is to have some impact on job performance. The appraisal workshop does not emphasize the stage of increased awareness and justification for the change except in so far as participants are offered a rationale. The workshop is not centrally concerned with philosophical issues relating to the justification of various forms of appraisal. There will be even larger differences in the stages of the learning process for which learning support is given within a programme. The education course emphasizes almost exclusively the development of critical understanding whereas the appraisal workshop provides support with the stages that link more closely to job performance. Programme managers must decide which components of learning support to include through certain activities and which to leave to the learners.

The fourth design step is, therefore, the crucial one of determining which activities or sets of activities may be used to address the components of learning support that it has been decided to include within the proposed programme. A brief assessment was given for each of the activities and sets of activities described in Chapters 3 and 4. Readers may wish to look back and assess for themselves in more detail which components of learning support are or are not addressed. Table 5.1 suggests which components of learning support form the major focus of the more substantial activities and programmes discussed in the earlier chapters. Many of them, such as action learning, may emphasize more than one component. It should be noted that some activities and programmes may also address certain components less fully than those that constitute their main emphasis. The analysis is necessarily crude as labels for a number of activities and programmes cover a wide variety of permutations. For example, the components covered by action learning differ according to whether or not the projects of participants from schools are based on management problems connected with their day to day work.

This analysis, although rough and ready, may help programme managers with the fourth step of selecting activities and sets of activities. Depending upon the aims of a programme being designed, the more of the necessary or advisable stages of the learning process that are covered by learning support the more likely it is that this support will result in informing or directly influencing performance in the job. A key to effective learning support is to design programmes that cover as many of the necessary stages of the learning process as is feasible within the parameters that have been set in the initial brief. Often it is possible to build up a programme of activities which focus on the transition between different stages in a way that matches the sequence within the learning process.

Table 5.1: The major focus of some activities and programmes
(note that many activities and programmes cover more components than their major focus)

Component of learning support forming major focus		Examples of activities and programmes
Diagnosis	(a) General behaviour	Counselling, learning styles analysis, personal journal, self development, stress management, action centred leadership, development and outdoor training, teambuilding with strangers
	(b) Job performance	Action research, conduct own case study, critical incident analysis, critical friendship, job enrichment, self development, being shadowed with feedback, personal journal, team building with working team, action learning, organization development, peer-assisted leadership, training courses and workshops, quality circles, consultancy
Critical understanding	(a) Research, professional knowledge, theory	Lecture and discussion, private study, self development, education course, open and distance learning, fellowship, peer-assisted leadership
	(b) Personal theories of action	Critical friendship, mutual support group, networking, personal journal, counselling, shadowing with feedback, action learning, education course, open and distance learning, fellowship, self development training courses and workshops, peer-assisted leadership, visits, action-centred leadership
Practical information	(a) General principles	Case studies, consultancy, self development, stress management, lecture and discussion, simulations, action learning, open and distance learning, peer-assisted leadership, training courses and workshops
	(b) Specific information for job tasks	Action research, consultancy, mutual support group, networking, shadowing, visits to schools, lecture and discussion, private study, self development, action learning, training courses and workshops
Skills	(a) Generic problem solving	Action research, quality circle, organization development, action learning

Skills	(b) Specific for job tasks	Simulations, skills training, open and distance learning, development and outdoor training for working teams, training courses and workshops
	(c) Specific for learning activity	Open and distance learning, action learning, peer-assisted leadership, quality circles
Integration into skilful performance	(a) Range of job tasks	Action research, job enrichment, job rotation (especially with mentor), being shadowed with feedback, peer-assisted leadership, teambuilding with working group
	(b) Specific job tasks	Peer coaching, expert coaching

Table 5.1 may be used as a first point of reference, together with the descriptions in the previous two chapters, in considering which activities or sets of activities may be worth including.

At this point let us note some of the patterns that a scan of Table 5.1 reveals. Many activities and sets of activities deal with the cognitive side of learning support, covering diagnosis, the development of critical understanding and provision of practical information. Fewer of these activities give strong support with the potentially powerful route to developing critical understanding through sustained study of research, professional knowledge and theory. Not many activities address squarely the learning of skills (especially the skills required to carry out learning activities), and fewer still focus upon integration into skilful performance in the job.

The thrust of the evidence reported in Chapter 2 is that support with the transition both from practical ideas to practice of skills and from practice into improvement in job performance may be highly beneficial in enabling participants to improve their individual and joint performance of management tasks in school. An important question for programme managers is whether they can find a way to include activities that support this end of the learning process within their programme design.

Readers may find it useful to use the framework of components of learning support to consider in more detail those components that may be addressed by some permutation of an activity or set of activities, as a basis for exploring whether supplementary activities may be desirable. A sample analysis of action learning as part of a more comprehensive education course is included in Table 5.2.

It will be seen that most components are addressed in some way. Incorporating action learning within an education course provides the opportunity for sustained work on developing critical understanding and for linking lectures, private study and inputs within the set to participants' own job experience. The decision that participants will undertake a project relating to a management problem within their normal work provides a basis for diagnosis during its

Table 5.2: **Sample analysis of activities covering components of learning support**

Component of learning support	Activity	Action learning within an education course
Diagnosis	(a) General behaviour	Feedback on behaviour in the set
	(b) Job performance	Project based in participants' own job
Critical understanding	(a) Research, professional knowledge, theory	Inputs from set adviser or experts brought into the set, participants may also draw on learning from lectures
	(b) Personal theories of action	Participants learn about others' personal theories through questioning, participants encouraged by questioning from others in the set to articulate their own personal theory and to question it themselves, lectures may provide link with research etc.
Practical information	(a) General principles	Inputs from set adviser or experts, private study
	(b) Specific information for job	Inputs from set adviser or experts, participants to gather information within their project
Skills	(a) Generic problem solving	Participants encouraged to explore and take managerial action to solve their problem within the project
	(b) Specific for job tasks	
	(c) Specific for learning activity	Set advisers give participants practice in asking questions and giving non-judgemental feedback on behaviour in the set
Integration into skilful performance	(a) Range of job tasks	Participants carry out management tasks in the project in school, with support (and pressure) from the set
	(b) Specific job tasks	

Table 5.3: A form for analysing components and activities

Component of learning support	Activity	
Diagnosis	(a) General behaviour	
	(b) Job performance	
Critical understanding	(a) Research, professional knowledge, theory	
	(b) Personal theories of action	
Practical information	(a) General principles	
	(b) Specific information for job tasks	
Skills	(a) Generic problem solving	
	(b) Specific for job tasks	
	(c) Specific for learning activity	
Integration skilful performance	(a) Range of job tasks	
	(b) Specific job tasks	

exploratory phase. The project entails managerial action in school to solve the problem, providing an opportunity to integrate what has been learned through a change in aspects of their job performance. However, support for integration in skilful performance is rather weak, consisting solely of participants' reports and the constructive questioning of their colleagues at the occasional meetings of the set. Should readers wish to try this approach to analysis of activities and the components of learning support they may serve, a blank form is included in Table 5.3.

So far we have considered how various activities may cover particular components of learning support. A most important criterion of a different kind for selection of activities is whether they may offer a structure for two or more colleagues from the same school to support each other's learning, whether as equals or not. As we saw in Chapter 2, learners may benefit from the support of colleagues in two main ways. First, colleagues are in a good position to give *technical* help with learning for job performance. There are activities for each of the five components of learning support where one person may help the other, whether by listening, discussing, observing and giving feedback or engaging in joint projects as part of both participants' managerial work. Second, colleagues may give *emotional* or moral support by encouragement, acting as a confidante, providing a source of constructive pressure, and generally demonstrating their interest in learners' success.

Colleagues may provide both technical and emotional support for learners within most activities. The potential may be greatest where colleagues give mutual support as peers since each may act as both learner and supporter for the other and each is likely to have empathy for the other's perceptions and feelings. Peer support need not necessarily imply that colleagues who give mutual support carry the same level of management responsibility. Whatever an individual's status and experience as a manager in school, she or he may have something to learn and may benefit from the support of other staff. For example, a deputy head and headteacher may establish a critical friendship where each observes the other in action and invites the other to reflect through non-judgemental feedback on what is observed. However, the greater the difference in status between colleagues the more difficulties they may have in perceiving each other as peers.

A fifth design step is to consider employing activities in which staff from the same school support the learning process. At this point it is also worth deciding whether the programme should therefore include induction activities to help staff to overcome any feelings of threat, to establish an appropriate learning agreement and to learn the skills entailed in providing support. Many activities and sets of activities may be used (and adapted where necessary) for mutual support between staff from the same school, including:

- peer coaching;
- shadowing;
- co-counselling;
- critical friendship;
- mutual support groups;
- networking;
- a joint project in school;
- a self development group;
- two or more members of staff attending the same programme, such as an external training course or workshop, an action learning set or a development and outdoor training experience;

- members of staff who do not participate in an external programme agreeing to provide support in school for a colleague who does attend;
- team building for staff with management responsibility who work together in school;
- an organization development programme where an external consultant works with the whole staff;
- setting up quality circles;
- a group of staff who conduct action research into their work as managers.

The structure and sequencing of learning support activities

The sixth design step is to consider the order in which activities may be employed to support the transition between stages of the learning process in the sequence that these stages are likely to occur. Each learning support activity is an experience for participants in its own right, which links more or less closely with their job experience. The aims of the great majority of learning support activities and programmes include promoting improvement in performance in the job, whether or not they give direct support for integration into a skilful performance. One way to centre learning support on managerial work in school is to base a programme upon one or more units or modules, each of which is extended by preparatory and follow-up work in the job. The structure of a module and its extension is portrayed in Figure 5.3. The same structure may be used for a wide variety of activities, whether they are part of external programmes or programmmes based in school.

Prior to the main activity or activities, participants prepare themselves with some form of diagnostic work in school. In the example of the school based workshop on appraisal that was described above, staff may be asked to write down their understanding of the aims of appraisal and to list their relevant expectations and concerns. This work is referred to in the first part of the main activity. In our example staff may be asked to exchange views in small groups and to report their shared concerns. Participants' experience is challenged and guidance for developing new practice is given through whatever components of learning support are covered in the main activity. In the final part, participants prepare for follow-up work in school by developing a personal or joint action plan. Staff may plan the first steps to introduce appraisal into their school and may each agree to complete a self appraisal form and discuss it in confidence with a colleague of their choice. Back in school participants implement their action plan, where possible with support. In the example each member of staff works with a colleague.

This simple modular structure may be repeated to build up a more substantial programme consisting of a sequence of modules. Between each main activity, participants take action in the job both to follow-up the previous activity and to prepare for the next. Figure 5.4 is an outline of an external training course based upon a modular structure. It shows how learning support modules, each extending into the job, may be added together to provide cumulative learning support

```
┌─────────────────────────────────────────────────────────────────────┐
│ Preparatory Action in the Job                                          │
│                                                                        │
│ o    prepare for learning support activity by diagnosis (e.g. through │
│      reviewing managerial work in school relevant to activity)        │
│                                                                        │
│ o    prepare for learning support activity by developing critical     │
│      understanding (e.g. by gathering the views of colleagues on a    │
│      topic to be addressed) or by reading a key text.                 │
└─────────────────────────────────────────────────────────────────────┘
                                    │
                                    ↓
┌─────────────────────────────────────────────────────────────────────┐
│ Learning Support Activity                                              │
│                                                                        │
│ o    link participants' job experience to content of activity, e.g. by│
│      discussion                                                        │
│                                                                        │
│ o    activity covering diagnosis/critical understanding/practical      │
│      information/skills related to the job                             │
│                                                                        │
│ o    support with learning to carry out the main activity, if          │
│      appropriate                                                       │
│                                                                        │
│ o    participants plan follow-up action in the job                     │
└─────────────────────────────────────────────────────────────────────┘
                                    │
                                    ↓
┌─────────────────────────────────────────────────────────────────────┐
│ Follow-up Action in the Job                                            │
│                                                                        │
│ o    participants implement action plan                                │
│                                                                        │
│ o    activity to support integration into skilful performance where    │
│      possible (e.g. peer coaching)                                     │
└─────────────────────────────────────────────────────────────────────┘
```

Figure 5.3:   The structure of a learning support module and its extension

for participants over a considerable period of time. Programmes developed by staff in school may follow the same modular structure.

Within this course design, each module may consist of between two and five days based at the training institution, separated by periods of between two and four weeks in school. The first module is a residential session which maximizes opportunities, both formal and informal, for participants to build the level of trust which is necessary if they are to support each other's learning within subsequent activities. The last module is designed largely as a preparation for the final medium term follow-up arrangements in school once the course is over.

Table 5.4 is a blank form for designing learning support programmes within a modular structure that includes preparatory and follow-up work in school. There is space for two modules but the framework may be extended for more substantial programmes. The timeline for each component of the modules may be worked out in terms of dates where these are pre-specified or according to the number of days required. The modular structure is divided into three parts:

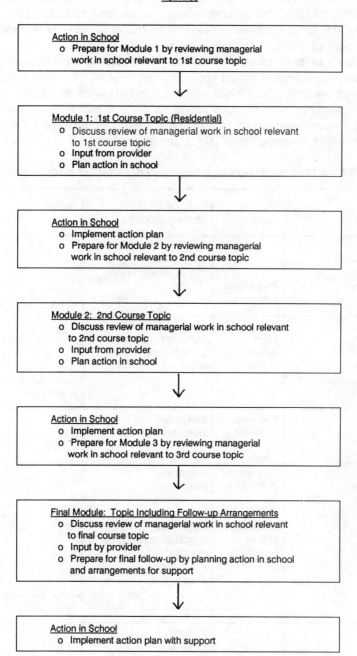

Figure 5.4:   Modular structure of an external training course

- preparatory work in school which includes activities covering diagnosis (e.g. an analysis of how each participant spent his or her time during one day) and, possibly, the development of critical understanding (e.g. by canvassing the judgements of colleagues on the usefulness of the school development plan);
- the main activity or activities, which may take place in the school or a variety of other locations, and may cover most components of learning support;
- follow-up work in school which focuses primarily upon integration into skilful performance (e.g. through action to solve a management problem or through peer coaching), with a secondary focus on providing a supportive climate which is conducive to taking action in school.

Table 5.4   A form for designing a sequence of extended modular activities

Timeline	Modular structure	Component of learning support	Activity
From (date/day no.) To (date/day no.)	Preparation in school	Diagnosis/ critical understanding	
From To	Module 1 Main Activity	Diagnosis/critical understanding/ practical information/ skills	
			action plan
From To	Follow-up in school	Integration into skilful performance	
From To	Preparation in school	Diagnosis/ critical understanding	
From	Module 2 Main activity	Diagnosis/ critical understanding/ practical information/ skills	
To			action plan
From To	Follow-up in school	Integration into skilful performance	

It is worth noting at this point that some activities commonly used for follow-up give little direct support with integration into skilful performance but may provide other valuable components of learning support. For example, mutual support groups or networks that arise from some external training courses may be useful for diagnosis and providing practical information. At the same time they may give emotional or moral support which helps learners to continue to work on improving their performance as managers. The relatively few activities that deal centrally with integration into a skilful performance were listed earlier in Table 5.1.

Resources for programmes

The seventh design step is to determine the resources that will be required to implement each activity within a programme and to consider the feasibility of implementing the design in the light of constraints posed by the availability of resources and the parameters for spending negotiated in the initial brief. Programme managers will need to consider the finance they require to secure the other kinds of resource. The budget for programmes developed by staff in schools may come from two main sources: firstly, the annual sum for staff development devolved by LEAs from the central government Grants for Education Support and Training (GEST) scheme; secondly, the LMS budget may possibly be used for certain resources such as materials that are used in learning support activities. For external programmes the initial brief will probably include an outline budget for resources that have to be bought in. At the initial design stage, it is important to consider how much flexibility there may be over the outline budget. Similarly it may be worth trying to predict any contingencies that may plausibly arise once the design is settled which would make an extra claim on the budget.

Any activity entails certain resources that may include:

- materials, ranging from notepads to training packs;
- equipment of various kinds, such as an overhead projector or video camera;
- one or more locations, whether in school or elsewhere;
- time, whether for group activities or personal reflection;
- facilities for travel and subsistence;
- people with specialist expertise as trainers or in substantive management topics;
- people to act as facilitators, who may or may not have relevant experience and expertise;
- people to cover participants' regular work in school.

When considering the choice of activities, resource questions are often central. As discussed earlier, some of the most powerful forms of learning support for school managers are labour intensive and, therefore, costly (although cost effective). Peer coaching, for example, requires time to be spent by people with expertise in preparing partners to observe and give feedback. Time must then be made available during the school day for each period of observation and outside lesson time for each feedback session. Where an activity or programme implies that staff must be released from their normal work, programme managers should consider not merely the resource cost but also the potential human cost in terms of potential for disruption to the normal work of pupils, as we saw in Chapter 1. Moreover, where cover is to be provided from within the school, disruption may be caused to the work of other staff.

Another key resource question relates to how much specialist expertise is necessary to lead or facilitate particular activities. Experts may be needed who are familiar with certain topics under consideration, such as LMS, development planning, marketing, or the law as it affects schooling.

Expertise may also be required in the training and learning methods implied by certain activities which it is not possible to acquire without experience in a training role. The NDC monitoring visits to courses designed to train heads and senior staff as trainers of their colleagues in other schools revealed how many participants developed expertise in particular topics rather than competence in using new methods. It is worth considering how far specialist expertise is required to lead activities effectively and, where this form of expertise is required, how it is to be obtained or developed.

The issue of expertise in methods applies not only to trainers and consultants but also to facilitators. Where it is intended that, say, heads and senior staff are to take on an unfamiliar role such as that of an action learning set adviser, it is important to consider what preparatory and ongoing support they may need. We cannot assume, for example, that a competent head will automatically be a competent trainer or facilitator without further learning. The model of learning for skilful performance put forward in Chapter 2 implies that trainers and facilitators learn through job experience and reflection in the same way as managers. Preparatory support can stimulate this process and ongoing support may help facilitators make the most of their opportunity to learn through their facilitation work.

Some means of checking through the resources needed to implement activities may be useful at the initial design stage. Table 5.5 illustrates the range of resources required for a one day visit to the LEA offices as part of an induction programme for new headteachers.

The only resources that are costed are those which are additional to the normal costs of running schools and LEAs and are specific to this activity. For instance, the salaries of participants and LEA staff are not included as it is unnecessary to do so for design purposes. Therefore a resource check need not cover all the costs of an activity. In the example the key costs are any claims upon the LEA's centrally retained budget for in-service training of school staff.

The financial cost and the list of resources offer pointers to programme managers about the feasibility and timing of the activity. If the activity is approved by the policy-makers, the list may be used in action planning to ensure that all the necessary resources are in place when needed. In our example, programme managers would need to arrange a meeting room with an overhead projector, to

Table 5.5:   Sample learning support activity resource check

Activity: Induction Day at LEA Office for new heads
Timing (no. days/dates): 1 day mid-week
No. participants: 10

Resources	Requirements	Estimated costing	Total cost (£)	Budget source
Materials	10 information packs for heads	10 × £3 each	30	LEA INSET
Equipment	Overhead projector	-	-	-
Location	Room in LEA office for meetings (9.30 – 12.30)	-	-	-
Travel	Participants' home to LEA office and return	10 × 20 miles at 30p/mile	60	LEA INSET
Subsistence	Coffee, lunch, tea	12 × £6 each	72	LEA INSET
Expertise	CEO, chief inspector, INSET co-ordinator, LMS co-ordinator, educational psychologist	-	-	-
Facilitators	Primary schools inspector, Secondary schools inspector	-	-	-
Cover	Estimate internal cover for 7 heads, supply cover for 3 heads for the day	3 × £70	210	LEA INSET
Other	-	-	-	-

Total cost: budget source A £372   (LEA INSET)
B £_____ (_____)
C £_____ (_____)

negotiate with their colleagues who are to provide inputs, to ensure that up-to-date information packs were available, and to make arrangements for lunch and refreshments.

Each activity within a major programme may be checked in this way and an assessment made of the feasibility of resourcing the full range of proposed activities within the parameters set in the initial brief. A blank resource check form is included in Table 5.6, should readers wish to try this approach.

Table 5.6: Resource check form for activities

Activity:
Timing (no. days/dates):
No. participants:

Resources	Requirements	Estimated costing	Total cost (£)	Budget source
Materials				
Equipment				
Location				
Travel				
Subsistence				
Expertise				
Facilitators				
Cover				
Other				

Total cost: budget source A £____ (LEA INSET)
                            B £____ (_____)
                            C £____ (_____)

Risks and safeguards

Fortunately, the evidence from evaluations suggests that most programmes are much appreciated by those who take part. However, as with school management tasks, the tasks of managing learning support programmes and providing learning support may be tackled more or less skilfully and their success depends not only upon the perceptions and actions of supporters but also those of participants. The gain from effective learning support for school managers is likely to be well worth the potential strain! While consideration of safeguards against things going wrong may not guarantee success, it helps to ensure that programmes are designed in such a way as to minimize risks. The eighth design step, therefore, is to consider possible risks and ways of safeguarding against them.

Let us pause to reflect upon the delicate nature of the interpersonal situations that many learning support activities represent. Learners bring expectations about an activity based upon their own past experience and assumptions about how they learn. They are fitting participation in the activity into their busy professional lives and are likely to wish not to have their precious time wasted by an experience which they find irrelevant, boring or incomprehensible. Those in a supporting role are equally busy and will often have an understanding of the activity based upon a different experience which is at odds, at least initially, with the perception of learners. They are likely to expect learners to suspend any disbelief in the learning potential of an activity and to participate fully in the opportunities provided. School managers tend to be in mid-career and to have enjoyed some success in their professional lives. The activity may pose an emotional threat where it challenges their assumptions about their level of competence in the job, questions their habitual ways of operating that have seen them through until now, requires them to undertake unfamiliar tasks where they do not feel competent, or exposes their weaknesses in front of colleagues from the same or different schools. Small wonder that participants may occasionally express misgivings or appear reticent to engage fully in learning opportunities.

Keys to safeguarding against the risks embodied in such delicate situations are meticulous planning which includes an eye to contingencies that may arise, regular monitoring and formative evaluation of participants' experience, and negotiation of an agreed code of behaviour that respects the rights and reflects the responsibilities of learners and supporters. Table 5.7 is an agony column which lists some of the common risks associated with learning support programmes for school managers, together with suggested ways of safeguarding against these risks. Readers may wish to refer to the list in considering the design of particular activities, their sequencing, procedures for negotiating a learning contract with participants, and the design of entire programmes. It may also be of use when action planning, as a reminder that certain tasks, such as negotiating a clear brief with external trainers or consultants, may need to be carried out in good time before the programme begins.

Table 5.7:   Some possible risks and suggested safeguards

Risks	Safeguards (as appropriate)
• Poor administration	• Detailed planning, well in advance, clearly designated organizer role, adequate secretarial support
• Programme budget overspent	• Clarify budget at the outset, keep back portion for contingencies
• Disruption to pupils' work	• Hold activities outside school day, use on the job activities
• External trainers or consultants fail to deliver what programme managers expect	• Give trainers or consultants a clear brief, check their credentials with others who have employed them
• Insufficient resources for participants, especially reading material	• Provide key reading material for each participant

• Participants unclear why they have been selected	• Make selection criteria explicit
• Participants' expectations do not match those of programme managers	• Specify what the programme will cover at the outset, brief prospective participants prior to acceptance on the programme, monitor progress regularly
• Facilitators have difficulty with this role	• Give facilitators a clear brief, offer preparatory and ongoing support
• Participants have a negative attitude towards the programme	• Negotiate a learning contract or agreement as a condition of participation
• Participants do not attend sessions regularly	• Negotiate a learning contract or agreement, ask participants to prepare their colleagues to cover their work if the programme requires their release
• Participants are dissatisfied but do not express this openly	• Regular monitoring and evaluation procedures
• Participants have difficulty with learning tasks as they do not have the necessary skills	• Provide preparatory and ongoing support with learning these skills
• Activities pose a psychological threat to participants	• Negotiate ground rules for activities, provide opportunities for peer support, give individual counselling
• Participants develop action plans but do not carry them out	• Negotiate a learning contract or agreement
• Participants' colleagues in school do not support them	• Negotiate learning contract or agreement with colleagues as well as participants, offer programme for two or more staff from the same school
• Participants have a series of learning experiences which they perceive as unconnected with their job	• Provide preparatory and follow-up work for each main activity, linking it with participants' work in school
• participants do not have sufficient uninterrupted time for study and reflection	• Plan sufficient periods of time away from the job for study and reflection
• Some participants have difficulty in attending evening or weekend activities due to family commitments	• Plan activities during the school day, provide creche facilities

Monitoring and evaluation

Although monitoring and evaluation are not part of the design of activities, it is essential to consider at the initial design stage what form these processes may take if full benefit is to be derived from them. Ideally, monitoring and evaluation should be planned as an integral component of the programme. A ninth design step for programme managers, therefore, is to consider how the progress of the programme will be monitored and how its quality and impact on participants' learning may be evaluated as rigorously as possible within the parameters that were set in the initial brief. It is not necessary to plan monitoring and evaluation procedures in great detail at this stage but it is important to be clear what may be possible and how these procedures may dovetail with learning support activities without disrupting them. Key considerations include the purposes of monitoring and evaluation; their major focus; who will be responsible for carrying them out; the timing of certain processes; and firming up an initial evaluation brief to be discussed with the policy-makers concerned with the programme.

The purpose of monitoring is to check how far planned processes and events are actually taking place. The purposes of evaluation may be threefold:

- to improve activities and programmes by assessing their quality and impact on participants' learning;
- to identify learning needs which may be met by future support activities, primarily within the present programme;
- to account for investment in the programme.

Formative evaluation concerns mainly the first two purposes. In the early stages of substantial programmes the major emphasis will tend to be upon the quality of participants' experience and their learning needs. Sufficient opportunities for feedback are necessary to enable programme managers to modify programmes whenever the evaluation implies that improvements could be made or particip-ants have learning needs that have not been met. For single activities or short programmes there will be little time for feedback while they are being carried out. The longer the programme, the more potential there is to adapt it in the light of feedback. However, feedback is only as good as the evidence that has already been gathered. Therefore it is essential to plan opportunities for this evidence to be gathered at frequent intervals, starting at the time the programme begins. It is possible to gather some evidence on impact during a programme based upon the modular structure outlined above. Participants may produce verbal or written reports on the work they have undertaken in school between major activities, whether as follow-up to a previous module or in preparation for the next.

Summative evaluation may refer to all three purposes. Towards the later stages of a long programme and once any activity or programme is over, it is possible in principle to gather evidence on how it has affected participants' learning. Where the aims include improving job performance, assessment of impact will focus on participants' management tasks and the effects of their attempt to fulfil these tasks. However, as we noted in Chapter 2, it is difficult and labour intensive to assess impact through measures which reach beyond collect-ing participants' views as there is a long causal chain from the performance of management tasks to improvement in pupils' learning. Obviously, summative evaluation of impact on performance depends upon gathering evidence after the programme is completed, meaning that arrangements for a review should allow ample time for this process and for a final report to be prepared.

The final review serves all three purposes, with a view to future initiatives for providing learning support. It enables programme managers and policy-makers to consider how improvements may be made in future programmes, how far the aims of the programme were achieved and what management development needs remain, and how far the programme was worth the investment put into it.

According to the purposes of the evaluation and the programme aims, it may focus upon the support offered through activities and upon participants' learning; their impact upon job performance; and the management of the programme in making use of the finances invested and in so far as it affects participants' experience. Once programme managers are clear about the purposes and focus of the evaluation, together with its scale as determined in the initial brief, they can work out what evaluation activities are likely to be involved. From there it will be possible to ensure that opportunities are provided within the programme design for these evaluation activities to take place.

How detailed programme managers' knowledge of the evaluation strategy will be at this stage depends upon the allocation of responsibility for carrying it out. For school based programmes the budget is unlikely to stretch to the employment of an external evaluator. Staff responsible for each programme or the person responsible for co-ordinating staff development are likely to take on the evaluation role. Their LEA may have standard evaluation forms and procedures which staff in schools are expected to adopt. In the case of substantial external programmes programme managers may be responsible for evaluation or it may be possible to employ an independent evaluator, perhaps a trainer from a higher education institution, a consultant or a seconded headteacher.

Important evaluation issues to be considered at the initial programme design stage are summarized in the checklist in Figure 5.5.

Where evaluators are not programme managers they should be appointed and given a brief far enough in advance to make it possible for evidence to be gathered, for example on programme planning or the process of identifying participants' needs, before the start of the programme. Unfortunately, it is all too common for evaluation to be added to programmes as an afterthought, with the result that it does not begin until the programme is well under way and valuable opportunities are lost for gathering evidence to fulfil the evaluation brief. Whatever the scale of a programme, it is important that all those directly involved are briefed about the evaluation and their co-operation secured before the attempt is made to collect evidence from them.

Evaluation activities can easily distract participants or disrupt the work of trainers. It is worth considering regular times (depending, of course, on the scale of the programme) when evidence may be gathered through, for example, administering a questionnaire, interviewing individuals or holding a plenary discussion. Times will also be needed when those responsible for learning support may receive formative feedback from evaluators which may inform their deci-

Issues to consider at the initial design stage (as appropriate):

1. Procedure for appointing and briefing evaluators

2. Procedure for briefing participants, trainers and programme managers about evaluation strategy

3. Availability of times during programme when evaluation evidence may be gathered from participants and those responsible for learning support

4. Meetings between evaluators and those responsible for learning support to receive formative feedback

5. Arrangements for liaison about evaluation between programme managers and policy-makers

6. Resources needed to carry out evaluation within parameters set

7. Form and scale of reports and their audience

8. Arrangements for protecting anonymity and for confidentiality.

Figure 5.5:   A checklist for initial consideration of an evaluation strategy

sions about any future modifications. At the same time it is also worth thinking about points when policy-makers may be informed about the interim findings of evaluation so that their approval may be gained for any changes to the programme and in order to give them an account of progress.

Other considerations that programme managers will need to sort out sooner rather than later include the resources that evaluation may require, especially secretarial support and cover; how comprehensive reporting will be, since the more extensive a report the more time and other resources will be required to compile it; any arrangements for protecting the anonymity of those involved in the programme and restrictions to be placed upon the dissemination of any report.

For substantial external programmes it should be possible, in the light of these considerations, to draw up an initial evaluation brief to be checked through with the policy-makers. The initial brief may include:

- a short statement of the evaluation purposes linked to the aims of the programme;
- an indication of who will be responsible for carrying it out;
- suggested points for evidence gathering and feedback;
- proposed times for liaison with policy-makers and for the final review;
- an indication of resources required;
- suggested arrangements for protecting anonymity and any recommended restrictions on the circulation of reports.

We have already mentioned that school staff are likely to carry out their own evaluation of programmes developed internally. Where there is a set of procedures for evaluating staff and management development work an evaluation brief may be no more than an agreement to follow the normal procedures.

The process of evaluation will be considered in greater detail in Chapter 7. Examples will be given of instruments used for evaluating school based and external programmes.

Action planning and implementation

Once the initial programme design and, where appropriate, the initial evaluation brief have been checked with the policy-makers, they may be revised if necessary as the basis for planning how to implement the programme and its evaluation. Many readers will have developed their own preferred approach to organizing events. One option is to adapt the sequence of action planning steps outlined in Chapter 3. Where the design process described above has been adopted, the revised design will give a clear idea of purposes, the general strategy and goals of action. The next programme management task is to work out what arrangements will have to be made, with whom and by when.

A popular strategy is to undertake a critical path analysis. The first step is to set out a timetable of relevant events from the present until the final review of the programme including activities and the arrangements that surround them, together with meetings for liaison with policy-makers. The next step is to work back from the time when an arrangement is to be in place to the deadlines by which the various tasks required to make the arrangement have to be completed. For example, the first module of an external programme may be a residential event over three days. It will be necessary to book a suitable venue, to revise the estimated numbers attending as the event draws near and inform the venue management of the final numbers. The critical path encompasses the dates of the residential module, the deadline for notification of final numbers, and the time by which programme managers hope to have booked the venue. This process may be repeated for other arrangements such as securing the services of external trainers, consultants or evaluators, disseminating publicity material, negotiating a learning contract with participants (see Chapter 3), or finding people who can act as facilitators and giving them preparatory training.

Critical paths for certain arrangements will be found to have implications for others, as in the case of an external programme where material is to be sent to prospective participants. It may be convenient to include in one mailing, say, details of the venue, an outline of the programme, a preparatory exercise to be carried out in school, and a short evaluation questionnaire concerning selection processes and participants' initial expectations. Evidently, arrangements must be made to ensure that each component is available by the time of the mailing.

It is possible to build up a fairly detailed timetable in this way that offers programme managers a series of prompts for action (which includes badgering

(Some tasks will vary between external programmes and programmes organised by staff in schools)

BEFORE

o   Liaise with those responsible for learning support activities and evaluation about their brief, participants' needs to be addressed, and details of administration

o   determine the timing and location of the programme to maximise accessibility to all prospective participants

o   communicate about the programme with all who are directly involved and acting in support (e.g. other staff in school), and with policy-makers

o   check arrangements for release of participants and facilitators

o   ensure that preparatory tasks for participants are provided

DURING

o   communicate with all parties directly involved and with policy makers

o   monitor what is happening to ensure that it is going to plan and to be able to respond to any need for immediate changes

o   ensure that formative evaluation is carried out and feedback provided

o   liaise with staff covering for participants, whether they are covering classes or undertaking management tasks as a planned management development activity

o   check that any arrangements to support participants after activities are implemented

AFTER

o   ensure that participants are given an opportunity to evaluate the quality of the programme and its anticipated impact

o   check that any arrangements for follow-up support are carried through

o   provide an account of any claims on the relevant financial budget

o   facilitate any procedures for evaluating impact of the programme

o   facilitate a review meeting between evaluators, policy-makers and programme managers

Figure 5.6:   A checklist of co-ordination tasks for implementing programmes

NDC CONSULTANCY WORKING AGREEMENT

Title of Programme: **Senior Management Team Review**

Client: (....) High School
                             (address)
                             (phone number)

Contact Person: (name)

NDC Contact Person   Mike Wallace
                             (NDC's address)
                             (NDC phone number)

Task: To facilitate a one day review of the work of the senior management team, with particular attention to whole school development and individual SMT roles.

NDC Fee   (£ ...) to be paid on completion of the tasks to be undertaken by the NDC. The client will provide lunch; the NDC will pay travel costs and supply materials.

The NDC undertakes to:

   o   attend a meeting of the SMT to consult members about the detailed aims and programme for the review

   o   prepare a provisional programme with supporting materials, focusing upon:

      (i)   progress with and plans for school development
      (2)   members' satisfaction with their existing roles and possibilities for change

   o   offer the provisional programme for comment at the beginning of the review

   o   facilitate group tasks and act as reporter.

The Client undertakes to:

   o   provide a suitable location with a flipchart and organise coffee and lunch

   o   prepare by asking members to consider the aims and programme for the review prior to the SMT meeting

   o   prepare individually for the review by

      (1)   listing items of concern in relation to school development

      (2)   checking through their job description and noting any gaps or areas of overload.

We agree that this is our understanding of our working agreement:

Signed _____ Client   date _____

        _____ NDC   date _____

Figure 5.7:   Extract from a working agreement

others if they have not met their deadlines) at key points before, during and after the programme. This timetable may also include periodic monitoring points to stimulate programme managers to check whether all arrangements are going to plan and to make modifications if necessary. At the same time it is worth considering contingencies that might arise, such as a trainer being unable to attend at the last moment, and to make outline plans for alternative arrangements. While it is often possible to delegate administrative tasks connected with a programme, it is equally important that one person takes overall responsibility for implementation so that, if necessary arrangements fail to be made, someone will be monitoring progress and be ready to take prompt action.

Some key co-ordination tasks that programme managers may have to carry out in overseeing the implementation of the programme are listed in Figure 5.6. Liaison tasks will vary with the size of the programme and the number of people involved in providing learning support. In comparison with external programmes, school based initiatives may require less extensive communication amongst those in management, training, facilitation and evaluation roles as one person will usually be responsible for more than one role and most people will be working in the same institution. Most of the tasks have already been mentioned in connection with programme design.

One task that deserves particular attention at the action planning stage is negotiation with prospective trainers, consultants and evaluators from outside the institution where programme managers are based. Arguably, they have a right to a clear brief in return for their obligation to do a thorough job. Initial negotiations and subsequent communication are greatly assisted if they are centred on a brief which, for accountability purposes, may be worth formalizing within a written agreement or contract. This contract should set out the obligations on both sides. A working agreement may usefully include:

- the title of the programme;
- the name of the client;
- the client's institutional base, address and phone number;
- the name of the client contact person;
- the name of the person whose services are being sought;
- her or his institutional base, address and phone number;
- a single sentence summary of the task;
- the fee to be paid, plus any reimbursement for travel, subsistence and materials;
- a list of the tasks to be undertaken to meet stated aims of the programme, with dates and times as appropriate;
- a list of the associated tasks to be undertaken by the client;
- a space for the signatures of both parties to the agreement and the date when the agreement was signed.

Figure 5.7 is an extract from a simple working agreement based on a form used by the NDC. A balance must be struck between developing a detailed agreement which inhibits modification in the face of unforeseen contingencies that arise and an agreement that is so imprecise that each party may come to a radically different interpretation of it.

The evaluation brief specifies the service required of evaluators and provides a set of parameters within which they agree to work. It firms up and extends the content of the initial brief in the light of consultation with the policy-makers. Detailed consideration of the evaluation brief is given in Chapter 7.

Examples of different programme designs are summarized in Chapter 6, together with a brief comment based upon the design steps suggested above. They suggest how a range of activities and sets of activities described in Chapters 3 and 4 may be incorporated in different programmes developed by staff in schools and those offered by external agencies.

6

SOME PROGRAMME DESIGNS

Many combinations of activities may be employed in developing a wide range of programmes to meet different management development needs. This chapter consists of summaries of the learning support activities incorporated in eight programme designs. The first four are based in a single school or a group of schools; the remainder are local or regional external programmes. They are fictional: a mixture of real experiences and ideas drawn from the literature discussed in earlier chapters. It must be stressed immediately that none of these designs is advocated as a model of perfection.

A comment upon each design gives brief consideration to:

- the needs that the programme is intended to meet;
- the purposes of continuing education that it serves (see Chapter 1);
- the components of learning support that it offers;
- some key resources;
- risks and safeguards;
- strategies for gathering evaluation evidence and feasible possibilities for improvement.

Readers may find it helpful to carry out a critical assessment of the strengths and weaknesses of these programmes in the light of the design considerations that have been highlighted earlier. A similar analysis could be applied to programmes in their own experience. Here are some questions that readers may like to bear in mind.

- What management development needs is the programme designed to meet and how far is it likely to succeed?
- Which principles of learning support are or are not followed?
- Which components of learning support are included and which are not?
- Which transitions between stages in the learning process are participants left to make without support?

- How far does the sequence of activities match the sequence of transitions between stages in the learning process?
- What content should be included in such a programme?
- What are the main resources required and how readily available are they likely to be?
- What are the chief risks in this type of programme and what safeguards might reduce these risks?
- How might evaluation evidence be gathered on the quality and impact of the programme?
- How might the programme be improved and what, if any, additional resources and risks might the improvement entail?
- Does this programme offer any useful ideas for the design of other programmes in readers' experience?

Programme 1: opportunities for job enrichment

Two examples will be described. In a large primary school staff are given new tasks in their present role. The deputy head takes on co-ordination of assessment within the National Curriculum and pupils' records. The head acts as a mentor to the deputy. Teachers who do not hold an incentive allowance assist experienced curriculum co-ordinators for mathematics, science and English who act as their mentors. When the head of a secondary school is seconded for a term, several staff are temporarily promoted: the senior deputy becomes acting head, a head of faculty becomes acting deputy, a deputy head of faculty becomes an acting head of faculty and a teacher on the main scale becomes acting deputy head of faculty. The other deputies act as critical friends for the acting head and as mentors for the acting deputy. The latter acts as a mentor for the acting head of faculty and so on.

Comment

Staff are supported in carrying out new management tasks which, except in the case of the primary deputy, are associated with a more substantial level of managerial responsibility than they currently hold. The programme is designed to meet the needs of staff who are interested in preparing for promotion by broadening their experience through tackling some of the tasks of a more senior post. It also provides a new stimulus for the present work of those taking on these tasks and the tasks of their mentors. Therefore it fulfills primarily the purpose of career development but also that of improving individual performance in the present job. The programme provides heads with an opportunity to develop a cadre of colleagues who may be eligible for internal promotion if a senior member of staff leaves.

There is considerable room for learning support with diagnosis through the challenge provided to those with extra responsibility and the feedback and advice given by mentors. Little support is given with developing critical understanding apart from articulation of the personal theory of the mentor, who is likely to be a strong source of practical information necessary to perform tasks, but possibly less strong on general principles. There is no focus on skills as such but tackling new tasks gives an opportunity to develop a problem solving approach to the job. Integration into a skilful job performance may be directly supported where mentors are able to observe the person for whom they are responsible at work and where they see its results. For example, a primary assistant curriculum co-ordinator may organize an in-service training session attended by the mentor, who subsequently offers feedback. Some indirect support may arise both from pressure to take action because of the expectation that new management tasks will be carried out and from the support of the mentor in solving problems over carrying out the relevant management tasks.

As an on the job activity with some close to the job support, this programme is comparatively light on resources. Time must be found for mentors to offer counselling. Mentors must develop relevant expertise, for instance in giving non-judgemental feedback or encouraging individuals to question their own performance.

There is a risk that learners may not be competent in carrying out their new tasks and mentors may be unhappy with such a situation since they have been and will once again take responsibility for these tasks. Mentors may be too busy to offer much counselling support. They may offer negative judgements on learners' performance that induce a feeling of resentment. The main safeguards are to establish a learning contract with agreement on the ground rules for both learner and mentor, and to timetable regular opportunities for learners and mentors to meet during non-contact time or outside the school day.

Evaluation evidence may be gathered after the initial briefing to check individuals' expectations, and during and after the programme. Learners may be asked to assess what they have learned through the job, how well supported they have been, and what results they have achieved. Mentors may be asked to assess their own work as mentors, learners' engagement in the opportunity to learn and their job performance.

The programme might be improved by employing an external trainer for, say, half a day to prepare mentors and learners for their role in counselling and to offer learners some guidance on developing a problem solving approach to their work. This arrangement would add to the cost of the programme.

Programme 2: team building for the senior management team

The example will be described of the senior management team (SMT) in a secondary school, although a similar programme may be employed for other working teams such as the teaching staff in a primary school. Members of the

SMT agree to offer and accept confidential, constructive feedback on their individual contribution to the work of the team. They work through the items that they think will be useful from a pack of distance learning materials such as those produced by the NDC for middle managers (Hall and Oldroyd, 1990). These materials include readings that highlight teamwork issues and activities which help members to diagnose their contributions to teamwork and plan ways of improving their individual and group performance. Members set aside one hour after school each fortnight to work on the material and allow up to twenty minutes to be spent reviewing their operation as a team at the end of the regular weekly SMT meetings.

The other staff are informed about the programme. They are invited to offer constructive suggestions through their head of faculty about ways in which the SMT could improve its teamwork in leading the management of the school. Staff are requested to consider whole team issues such as communication between SMT members or the degree of overlap between members' roles, and are requested to refrain from making personal comments about individuals.

Comment

The programme is designed to meet both individual needs to carry out tasks which contribute to the work of a team and the group need to collaborate effectively in carrying out joint tasks. It fulfills the dual purpose of improving individual performance and improving group performance.

Diagnosis is supported through feedback from other SMT members, the distance learning exercises and feedback from other staff. There is some emphasis upon critical understanding. The materials offer some evidence from research and professional experience inside and outside education, together with conceptual frameworks and practical activities derived from them. SMT members are invited to articulate and challenge their personal theories of action through the activities and the feedback they offer each other in SMT meetings. Some practical information is given, mainly in the form of general principles. While SMT members are encouraged to take action to solve problems with their teamwork, the materials do not provide direct support with the learning of skills. Support for integration into a skilful performance comes from mutual observation in SMT meetings and feedback on performance of tasks representing individual contributions to the joint work of the team. Encouragement and pressure to take action may result from the involvement of all SMT members in the initiative.

The main resources required include non-contact time and time after school for team building sessions, plus enough sets of distance learning materials for all SMT members.

There is a risk that a psychological threat may be posed to individuals, possibly those heads who feel their authority may be undermined or less senior colleagues who fear that their promotion chances might be jeopardized by the exposure to the head of their personal weaknesses. Other staff may be unwilling to give candid, constructive feedback for a similar reason. One safeguard is to ensure that a mutual learning contract with appropriate ground rules is agreed at the outset and that individuals are invited to challenge those who transgress. SMT members may find themselves too busy with high priority management tasks to spend time on focusing on learning. A safeguard may be to agree to a flexible approach to the programme, checking progress regularly and being willing to postpone it and to continue when time permits.

The quality and impact of the programme may be evaluated by gathering evidence during and after it. Evaluation may focus on SMT members' initial expectations and concerns and their perceptions of the team building experience and their performance as a team. Rough indicators might include how much work is dealt with in SMT meetings or how many important decisions are made. Heads of faculty and pastoral heads could be asked at the beginning and end of the programme about any evidence they have on the level of performance of the SMT (such as the number of recent instances of poor communication).

The programme is introspective. An improvement may be for one or more SMT members to observe an SMT meeting at another school and to report back to colleagues. An obvious difficulty with this proposal is the possibility that with increasing competition between schools imposed by central government, hostility may be engendered by the possibility of industrial espionage! One way out might be to go to a school which is sufficiently far away not to be in competition for pupils. A second improvement may be to book a venue for one or more of the after school sessions in which SMT members may enjoy comfortable surroundings and where they may be free of interruptions.

Programme 3: a mutual shadowing programme for headteachers

An initiative taken by a cluster group of primary schools will be described, although a similar programme may be developed by a secondary school consortium or a pyramid of feeder primary schools and a secondary school. Participation in the exercise is voluntary for heads. They arrange specific tasks for their deputies to undertake while taking over the headship role as a planned development exercise. The first workshop takes place in the afternoon and the other two workshops take place in one of the schools after the pupils have gone home. An external trainer conducts the first workshop, explaining what is involved, gaining heads' agreement about confidentiality and arranging for them to pair up for the first shadowing exercise. Participants are shown an observation schedule and practise observing by watching a video of a primary head at work in various situations and then discussing the notes they have made. They are introduced to the ground rules of non-judgemental feedback and practise asking questions on the basis of their notes to stimulate reflection. Each person in a pair observes her or his partner for a day and gives feedback after school.

Participants come back together for a second workshop with the trainer where they review their experience of the shadowing technique and of being shadowed and receiving feedback. The trainer demonstrates a technique for recording how the person being shadowed uses his or her time. Participants practise the technique by watching another video of a head in school. Pairs undertake a second mutual shadowing exercise where, before the school day begins, the partner being shadowed makes a timetable of the tasks that are planned to be carried out. The observer gives factual feedback on what actually took place. The person who has been shadowed explains why any discrepancies occurred and considers how his or her use of time may be improved. Each pair conducts a third mutual shadowing exercise, using the techniques that have been learned. The focus is upon the efforts of the person being shadowed to improve the use of time.

At the final workshop pairs review their experience of the technique and consider what they have learned about their managerial performance. They plan action to improve their performance and to monitor their use of time. The trainer invites the heads to consider how they may use the techniques of observation and feedback in monitoring and supporting the development of their staff.

Comment

The programme is designed to meet the needs of experienced heads to improve their use of time, to reduce their sense of isolation in the job, and to learn some observation and feedback techniques that they may subsequently use in fulfilling their responsibility for the development of their staff. Thus the programme serves the purpose of improving individual job performance.

Support is provided for diagnosis through the feedback participants receive and their reflection on the performance of the partner whom they have observed. The discussions between partners after shadowing in school and in the workshop sessions promote critical understanding but it is confined to the articulation of personal theories of action. Practical information is offered on how to conduct the learning task of observing and giving feedback, and participants pick up practical tips and some general principles from what they observe and hear. Participants receive support for learning the skills of observation and feedback. Some support is given for integration into a skilful performance through the repeated shadowing exercises where individuals' efforts to improve their performance in the light of earlier feedback are observed and feedback offered. The expectations of their partner may encourage heads to take action during the shadowing exercise.

Resources required may include supply cover to enable heads to attend the initial workshop and for the three days when they are shadowing. Time is also needed after school for feedback and workshops. The trainer may charge a fee.

Heads may feel threatened by the prospect of being observed by another head whom they may perceive as a competitor or as less competent than themselves. The main safeguards are to negotiate at the first workshop a learning contract and appropriate rules of procedure for observation, feedback and respecting confidentiality. It may be helpful for an external trainer who is perceived to be impartial but supportive to facilitate this negotiation. Staff and parents coming into school may be put off by the presence of the shadowing head. Heads may gain the agreement of staff to support the shadowing exercise and ask parents who come to see them whether they mind the presence of a shadow. Another risk is the possibility that observers may be tempted to make judgements in giving feedback, which may be minimized by careful preparatory training and a review after the first shadowing exercise. Finally, heads may find themselves too busy to take a day away from school to shadow their partner. The learning contract may help heads to make the shadowing work a high priority. Flexibility may be needed to complete the mutual shadowing exercises between workshops which should be separated by several weeks.

Evaluation evidence on the quality and impact of the shadowing experience may be collected from participants and the trainer at each workshop and, possibly, through a review at a subsequent meeting of the cluster group.

The programme could be improved by further shadowing exercises for each pair. Heads may benefit from provision of a framework for interpreting what they observe and the feedback they receive (see peer-assisted leadership in Chapter 4). The programme could be designed to include heads shadowing volunteers among their staff.

Programme 4: an in-service training day on stress management

The whole staff of a primary or a secondary school use one of the five annual non-contact days to review how they experience stress in their work outside the classroom and to consider feasible ways of reducing this stress. We will use the example of a secondary school. The day is organized by the staff development co-ordinator. Before the day, members of staff are asked to consider how stressful they find their involvement in school management, whether as a main scale teacher or a member of staff with major management responsibility, and to identify factors that make them feel stressed in their professional and personal lives.

The content of the day is the responsibility of an LEA educational psychologist, who begins the first session by setting out rules of procedure for discussion and by giving out sets of handouts. Participants are asked to respect confidences, to focus upon their personal experience of stress and to refrain from blaming other people for the situations that have stimulated their stress response. They discuss in small groups what makes them feel stressed and receive a lecture in which the concept of stress, its causes and relevant research findings about stress in teaching are explored. The educational psychologist invites staff to form confidential, critical friendships for stress management, consisting of no more than three people. The intention is for each partner to agree to confide in and give support to the other. Participants then form pairs or trios where they discuss ways in which they might avoid stress in their personal lives and their work in school. Individuals identify a critical incident from their involvement in managing the faculty, the pastoral system or the school which they have found stressful. They consider how they might react differently to such situations if they occur again and also consider how far their actions might help to prevent similar incidents from happening in the future.

The educational psychologist gives a second input on the link between stress experienced outside school and behaviour inside school and stress related to school management. Suggestions are made about ways of reducing stress. In their pairs or trios participants identify how their actions in contributing to school management may inadvertently give rise to a stress response in others and consider whether they may operate differently. Each person works out a personal action plan for reducing his or her experience of stress and that of others in contributing to the management of the school. Partners agree to confide in each other if they experience heavy stress in the future.

Comment

The workshop relates to the need of individuals to improve the way they contribute to the tasks of managing the school by avoiding a stress reaction and increasing their sensitivity to the effects of managerial action upon others. Its purpose is to improve individual job performance in contributing to the managerial performance of the whole staff.

Several opportunities are given for diagnosis before and during the workshop, and critical friendships may promote diagnosis afterwards. The lectures give limited support for the development of critical understanding through reference to research, professional knowledge and theory, and discussions enable individuals to articulate their personal theories. However, the emphasis is upon how to manage stress rather than upon a critical understanding of the nature of the phenomenon. The lectures and handouts provide practical information in the form of general principles and practical tips. No support is given for practising the skills of stress management. Indirect help with integration into a skilful performance is offered through the supportive climate engendered by the critical friendships.

Resources include the services of the educational psychologist, handouts, an overhead projector and lunch. A large space is needed which can accommodate all the staff, together with smaller spaces for groups and pairs or trios.

Perhaps the most obvious risk is that individuals may openly identify the direct causes of their stress response as the behaviour of others who are present, thereby no doubt inducing a fair dose of stress in them! This risk may be reduced by employing a workshop leader who is likely to be perceived as a person with authority, and who sets out the rationale for rules of procedure, lists the rules and insists that they are respected. Stress is an emotional factor affecting and affected by the way in which management tasks are carried out. A second risk is that participants will not be capable of making changes to their behaviour without further support with the skills embodied in techniques for stress reduction.

Evaluation evidence may be gathered at the end of the workshop to assess its quality, comparing participants' expectations and concerns with the experience

they received. A short questionnaire a month afterwards would enable participants to give an indication of its impact.

A key improvement would be to provide skills training, perhaps with a follow-
up session after school a month after the workshop. It may be possible to include
skills training within the workshop if the leader could be supported by facilitators with expertise in stress management techniques.

Programme 5: a short external workshop on managing assessment

This is a workshop for staff with major responsibility for assessment in primary
schools. A similar workshop could be organized for the secondary phase. It is a
one day programme held at a teachers' centre and led by an LEA adviser as part
of an LEA cascade training strategy. Headteachers are asked to send one person
from their school who has responsibility for assessment; to help them afterwards
to disseminate information to colleagues; and to provide some non-contact time
for them to work on the school's assessment policy and support teachers who
have to administer standard assessment tasks. Prospective participants are asked
to agree to carry out preparatory work and follow-up tasks in school. They
prepare by writing a one page review of progress with assessment of the National
Curriculum, bringing any relevant school policy document, arranging for dissemination to their colleagues in school, and asking a colleague to give informal
support by acting as a critical friend.

The LEA adviser arranges for several advisory teachers to act as group facilitators and briefs them before the workshop starts. In small groups, assessment co-
ordinators exchange with each other about progress and their current concerns
in carrying out their management tasks. They receive a lecture from the adviser,
who introduces a pack of assessment materials. Participants discuss how they will
use these materials to raise the awareness of staff about the implications of
assessment within the National Curriculum for current practice, develop or revise an assessment policy, and work to implement it. Participants revise or write
a short draft policy which covers issues raised by the adviser, and draw up an
individual action plan for their work in disseminating information, negotiating
and implementing the policy. They are asked to discuss both documents with
their headteacher on their return to school. Participants are encouraged to network with colleagues from their discussion group and regularly to consult the
member of staff in the school who has agreed to act as a critical friend about the
tasks of managing the introduction of assessment.

Comment

The programme is designed to help staff meet their legal obligation to assess the
National Curriculum by offering support for co-ordinators with the management
tasks of disseminating information, developing an assessment policy and leading
its implementation. The purpose served by the programme is to influence the

performance of teaching staff in the area of assessment through the managerial performance of co-ordinators.

Participants are given support with diagnosis through the preparatory activity and group review during the workshop, and are encouraged to seek the help of a critical friend in school to help them plan action in the future. The emphasis of the lecture and the materials is mainly upon general principles and detailed information necessary to perform the tasks of managing the curriculum, rather than upon critical understanding. They are given brief opportunities to practise the skills of policy writing and action planning. No direct support is given for integration into a skilful performance but supportive conditions are fostered through the requests to headteachers, the idea of consulting a critical friend and the encouragement to network with colleagues from other schools.

Resources required include the materials, the venue and its facilities such as an overhead projector, lunch, expertise for the input, facilitators for the workshop, support from the head and a colleague in school, money to reimburse travel expenses, administrative support, and supply cover.

The withdrawal of staff from school for a day may risk causing disruption to pupils. Participants may fail to take action in school, although action planning, the requests to heads and the interest of a critical friend will help to ensure that there is support and pressure to do so. The lecture and materials may be difficult for participants to relate to their existing knowledge and experience, but the preparatory work and group discussions are intended to help them tune into the content of the input. Facilitators may have difficulty with their tasks, but the briefing session should help them to clarify what they have to do.

Evaluation evidence may be collected at the beginning of the workshop to check expectations and concerns. At the end, participants may be asked to assess the quality of the experience and indicate what they plan to do in school. A month after the workshop they, their headteachers and critical friends may be invited to complete a short questionnaire about what has been achieved as a result of the workshop.

Plausible improvements include the possibility of advisory teachers going into school after the workshop to act as consultants. A longer workshop could have provided practise in the skills of making a presentation within a dissemination exercise, and observing and giving constructive feedback to colleagues who are learning to administer the standard assessment tasks.

Programme 6: a regional training course for heads of faculty

This example is a course for heads of faculty in secondary schools within several LEAs. A similar programme could be offered for curriculum co-ordinators in primary schools. The programme is offered by a higher education institution and has been developed in consultation with representatives from LEAs in the region. A letter is sent to secondary schools in the participating LEAs inviting them to select two heads of faculty who agree to support each other through acting as critical friends and by undertaking peer coaching. They are requested to seek the commitment of staff in their faculties to support the programme, which will include the observation of faculty meetings. The letter of invitation states that pairs of nominees will be accepted on a first come, first served basis. The focus of the programme is upon the tasks of managing teaching, learning and assessment within the National Curriculum. Prospective participants are asked to accept responsibility for their part in a learning contract and to prepare by canvassing and noting down the opinions of staff in their faculty about progress with meeting the requirements of the National Curriculum and assessment, and their views about how the faculty should be developed to meet targets set out in the current school development plan. Figure 6.1 offers a summary of the programme structure.

There are four modules, the first of which is a three day residential exercise located at the training institution's conference centre. The remaining modules each last one day, are held a month or so apart from each other, and are located in the training institution. For the first module experienced heads of faculty who have been given preparatory training act as group facilitators. During this module pairs are split up and exchange information in cross-LEA groups about their context with those from other LEAs. Pairs come back together to share the outcomes of their preparatory work within new cross-LEA groups. This experience is designed to facilitate the development of trust within and between pairs. They receive a couple of lectures from an LEA adviser on managing the curriculum and its assessment, and use the accompanying handouts to consider the implications of issues raised for their work as faculty managers. Participants are encouraged to get to know those whom they have not met before through informal socializing between sessions.

A trainer gives an input on policy-making and strategic planning, offering a framework for developing written policies and a planning and decision-making model based upon research findings. Participants try applying these tools in a simulation exercise of a fictional faculty and receive feedback from the facilitators.

In a second input they are introduced to the notion of peer coaching, given materials explaining the process and provided with checklists for observation and feedback. The trainer demonstrates good practice in observation through a role play exercise where the facilitators take the part of faculty staff in a planning meeting. Afterwards the trainer gives non-judgemental feedback in an interview with the person acting the part of the faculty head (see Chapter 3 for details of peer coaching). Participants work in trios, one observing and giving feedback to the other two who attempt to solve a simulated faculty planning problem together. Each member of the trio has a turn as peer coach. Facilitators monitor participants' use of the technique and offer feedback to observers.

Participants plan three areas of action in school. First, they consider how they will work on developing existing faculty policy. Second, each pair works out an arrangement for peer coaching where partners observe part of a faculty meeting.

Module Structure	Activity
Preparation in school	Consult faculty staff about National Curriculum and assessment and development of faculty
Module 1 (3-day residential)	Review preparatory consultation exercise, inputs on managing curriculum and assessment, policy-making and strategic planning, introduction to peer coaching, action planning
Follow-up in school	Developing faculty policy, peer coaching by observing a planning meeting and giving feedback
Preparation in school	Consult faculty staff about meetings
Module 2 (1 day)	Review experience of peer coaching and strategic planning, review preparatory consultation exercise, input on managing meetings, practise observing meetings, action planning
Follow-up in school	Peer coaching by observing faculty meeting and giving feedback
Preparation in school	Review the monitoring of faculty staffs' work in the classroom
Module 3 (1 day)	Review what learned about effective meetings from peer coaching exercise, input on classroom observation, practise classroom observation, action planning
Follow-up in school	Second peer coaching exercise observing faculty meeting and giving feedback
Preparation in school	Peer coaching by observing teaching and giving feedback
Module 4 (1 day)	Review peer coaching on classroom observation. Input on improving monitoring within faculty, action planning
Follow-up in school	Action to improve monitoring within faculty, continuation of peer coaching

Figure 6.1:   Outline of a regional training course

The focus of the observation is to be each faculty head's leadership of planning and budgeting for the modification of courses for pupils in order to take into account the demands of the National Curriculum. Formative feedback is to be given after each meeting to the faculty head who led it. Third, in preparation for the second module each partner reviews the structure and frequency of regular meetings among faculty staff. He or she seeks the opinion of faculty colleagues about the effectiveness of these meetings and ways in they could be improved (or in some cases, abandoned). Thus between the first and second modules pairs both follow-up the topic they have addressed and prepare for the next through action in their job as faculty heads.

A similar sequence is followed for the remaining three modules, building competence in peer coaching to support learning to improve the performance of management tasks in school. The second module begins with a review of what has been learned about strategic planning. It focuses primarily upon designing a structure of meetings and upon managing them. Participants are introduced to ways of understanding behaviour in meetings and research based strategies for analysing it. Pairs practise using observation schedules for analysing interpersonal behaviour. They will use these schedules in school to observe each other leading a faculty meeting and to offer feedback within the framework of the schedule.

Participants prepare for the third module by reviewing the means used within the faculty to monitor teachers' work in classrooms and its outcomes. They discuss what they have learned about effective behaviour in managing meetings and move on to consider techniques for classroom observation. After the third module pairs carry out a second observation on each partner's behaviour in managing meetings. They also observe each other teaching and give feedback to follow up what they have covered in the third module. This exercise is also designed as preparation for the final module where the monitoring topic will be continued. During this module they consider how such an approach to classroom observation might be introduced into the work of department heads within the faculty. At the end of the final module pairs plan their strategy for introducing classroom observation and for continuing to give each other peer coaching support.

Comment

This programme is intended to meet participants' needs to improve the way they carry out their management tasks as faculty heads, especially in dealing with changes following from central government reforms. Its purpose is to improve individual job performance as a means of influencing indirectly the performance of a group of staff.

Multiple opportunities are offered for diagnosis through preparatory reviews, inputs and peer coaching (both observing another manager at work and receiving feedback). There is limited attention to developing critical understanding, largely confined to the application of research and theory rather than questioning the practice it prescribes. General principles are put forward and detailed information necessary for the performance of management tasks is provided. Support is offered in practising specific skills required for management tasks and in the tasks of peer coaching. Repeated use of peer coaching supports integration into a skilful performance of particular management tasks.

The programme requires supply cover to release participants and facilitators. Other resources include the venues; finance for travelling expenses; subsistence; expertise in training, the substantive topics and facilitating; the training institution's charges; and non-contact time and time after school for the peer coaching work and preparatory tasks.

A key risk in such a complex design which is intended to provide a cumulative experience is that individuals may not attend all sessions. In addition, heads and faculty staff may not give support to participants for the work in school that is an integral component of the programme. A safeguard is to negotiate a learning agreement with participants, their faculty staff and heads. Some disruption to pupils may arise from days spent by participants away from school, yet the alternative of holding sessions outside school hours may deter those with family commitments. Where schools are able to develop strong links with particular supply teachers or to provide some cover from within the faculty, disruption to pupils may be minimized.

Evaluation evidence may be collected through a short questionnaire during each module of the programme. Participants may be sent a questionnaire some months after the final module where they are asked to comment upon the impact upon themselves and their partner. Heads may also be asked to comment on the work of their faculty heads, referring to tasks achieved in managing the faculty.

The programme would benefit from being longer, with further modules covering more topics, providing opportunities for greater repetition of peer coaching exercises in relation to particular tasks. The programme could be designed to cascade the peer coaching model through pairs learning to act as trainers, facilitating the learning of other colleagues in school to engage in peer coaching.

Programme 7: an action learning programme for managers

We will take the example of an action learning programme for managers which includes participants from industry and commerce and deputy heads from secondary schools. The programme is offered by a business school. Two participants from each organization attend the programme, the first session of which lasts a day. Eight subsequent half day meetings of the action learning sets are held at monthly intervals. All meetings take place during the school day and are based at the business school. The prospective participants' senior managers are asked to support their efforts in tackling a personnel problem connected with their normal work. Participants are asked to prepare by identifying a difficult problem or issue that affects their individual work, which they have the authority to resolve, and which it is feasible to deal with in the next nine months or so. The problem forms the basis of the action learning project. In the case of the deputy heads, problems might be to resolve a dispute among heads of department over their share of the timetable and staffing or to develop a way of integrating LMS with the existing approach to strategic planning.

During the morning of the first meeting participants receive a lecture on Revans's theory of action learning and an outline of the main components of the process. They are asked to join sets which are made up of pairs of participants from three organizations, facilitated by an experienced set adviser. Each table at lunch is occupied by a set with its set adviser. In the afternoon the set adviser introduces the rules of procedure and asks for all members to respect the confidentiality of what will be discussed in the set. Each participant in turn describes her or his management problem. The set adviser checks that each problem lies within the definition that participants have been asked to follow. After each problem has been outlined it is explored through questions from other members of the set designed to stimulate reflection by the person who presented the problem. Members plan action in the workplace to find out more about the nature and causes of the problem they initially identified.

In the time between each set meeting participants work on their project in the workplace. Pairs from each organization are encouraged to support each other as critical friends. Where appropriate, they observe each other at work on the project (for example, when a deputy head chairs a meeting of heads of department) and give confidential feedback.

At each meeting of the set they report on progress and outstanding issues and are questioned by other members of the set. They hear about the progress of other members and question them to stimulate their thinking about the nature of and possible solutions to the problem. Where a member asks for advice, others may offer ideas based on their own experience. The set adviser gives a short input during each meeting related to problem solving and to personnel management issues. She or he also points to the ways in which set members are learning both through their project and from each other within the set. The early meetings focus upon investigating members' problems in depth. Later the emphasis shifts towards identifying, implementing and evaluating action to solve the problems. The final meeting consists mainly of a review of what has been learned. Pairs plan how they may continue to support each other in the workplace afterwards and plan any action that they may wish to undertake in connection with the present or a future project.

Comment

The programme is designed to meet individual managers' need to improve their performance in solving important problems in their present work. It serves the purpose of improving individual job performance.

Opportunities for diagnosis are offered through feedback on participants' behaviour in the set, the analysis of the management problem, support from their partner in the workplace, and the stimulation of hearing about the management problems of managers in different fields. Any development of critical understanding comes largely from the articulation of participants' personal theories of action, with some input from the set adviser who may draw upon research, professional knowledge and theory. Some practical tips may be offered by set members on request but the main emphasis is upon participants developing their own ideas for tackling their management problem. Support is given with skills involved in working effectively as a member of an action learning set and in solving problems. The only direct support for integration of the approach to problem solving into their job performance may come from any observation and feedback given by participants' partner in school. However, pressure and support for taking action is offered by the partner and other set members.

Some supply cover may be required to enable deputy heads to be released from their duties in school. Finance will be needed to reimburse travel expenses. The business school charges for the services of experienced set advisers, a venue with a meeting room for each set, and meals.

Risks include the pair of participants being unwilling to support each other in school, feeling uncomfortable about discussing their management problem in front of a colleague, or not having the backing of their headteacher when attempting to implement a solution to the problem. The main safeguard is to establish a learning agreement between deputies and the head as a condition of attendance and for the deputies to consult the head regularly about their progress and plans with the management problem, taking her or his views into account.

Evaluation evidence may be collected before, during and after the programme, focusing upon the quality of the experience of working in an action learning set and progress with the management problem. The head or other staff may be invited give an assessment of the impact of the programme upon the deputies' managerial work, both in connection with the problem and their general approach to solving problems in their day to day work.

The programme is weak on developing critical understanding, which could be added through more inputs, along the lines of the education courses incorporating action learning to which we referred in Chapter 4. A stronger link with other colleagues in the school could be established, possibly through preparing participants to act as set advisers for an action learning set in the school made up of volunteers from the staff.

Programme 8: a substantial modular education course

This programme is offered by a university and provides a range of options for primary and secondary school staff and school administrators. The course is accredited at Master's degree level. Most modules may be studied full-time, giving an opportunity for sustained reflection. There is also a range of modules which may be studied part-time at the university, and distance learning modules with the possibility of local tutorial support. Participants' essays and dissertation are assessed on the basis of their ability to demonstrate critical understanding of research, professional knowledge and theory and the ability to use this knowledge to interpret practical management situations. Participants are encouraged, where possible, to conduct action research into their own practice as managers, to analyse their experience, drawing upon the literature they have studied during other parts of the programme, and to write up an account of their action research as their dissertation. The main activities are lectures, plenary discussions and seminars, many of which include handouts. Participants have access to a large library consisting mostly of books and journals, which vary from the practical to the highly abstract. They are given tuition in study skills and research methods, both of which may be applied in their dissertation.

Comment

This education programme is designed to meet individuals' need to develop critical understanding of educational management and its social and political context, to articulate and justify their managerial beliefs and values, and to enable them to make more fully informed judgements in their work as managers. It serves mainly the purpose of developing professional knowledge but gives opportunities to take managerial action informed by this knowledge. For participants who take advantage of these opportunities the programme may also serve to a lesser degree the purpose of improving individual job performance. Since the criteria for selection to senior management posts often include professional qualifications, the programme may contribute towards career development for many participants.

Where participants analyse aspects of their own practice, either through essays or action research, learning support includes diagnosis. However, by far the greatest emphasis for all participants is upon developing critical understanding through reflective study of research, professional knowledge and theory. They are also encouraged to articulate their personal theory of action and to question and justify their managerial beliefs and values as they become increasingly informed about other perspectives and a wide range of evidence through their reflective study. In modules which address management tasks such as appraisal or staff selection, participants may learn about general principles and pick up a small amount of detailed information necessary for performing the job. Support with the learning of skills is given in the areas of critical analysis of practical management issues and academic study and, for those who conduct small scale research into their managerial work, the skills of investigation. Participants who conduct action research are supported in developing the skills entailed in a problem solving approach to their job. Support for integration into skilful performance is offered to those who take managerial action to solve the problem raised within their action research. No direct support is given with integration of participants' enhanced capacity for analysis and critique into the skilful performance of making informed judgements in their managerial work.

Key resources include the facilities of a university, such as a library, and academic staff with expertise in the relevant areas of research, professional knowledge and theory, and expertise as teachers. Distance learning modules require the provision of extensive study materials. The services of the university command a fee.

Possibly the most commonly stated risk is that participants will develop their critical understanding but that it will not be linked to their managerial performance. It was argued in Chapter 2 that this link is bound to be more or less indirect since critical understanding is not necessary (although desirable) for the performance of management tasks. It is possible to encourage participants to employ their critical understanding and ability to analyse in their job by undertaking a project which involves critical analysis in solving their managerial problems, as in the case of action research. We saw in Chapter 4 how education programmes which include action learning also make a deliberate attempt to forge this link. A second risk for participants who are unable to study any modules on a full-time basis is that they will not have a sufficient span of uninterrupted time to study topics in depth. Other risks are common to some of the programmes discussed above and the safeguards mentioned there apply in this case (for example, poorly prepared lectures or difficulties with access to books that are in heavy demand).

In the past, evaluation of education courses has been largely restricted to their impact upon participants' learning about research, professional knowledge and theory and their capacity for critical analysis. It is straightforward to evaluate the quality of the teaching through questionnaires at the end of taught sessions. Since the impact of developing critical understanding upon job performance is likely to be diffuse, the evaluation of long-term impact may have to rely upon self reporting by past participants. Where individuals undertake action research it is possible to assess its impact on their management performance through self reporting corroborated by the views of other staff.

Improvements depend upon the purpose of the programme. To the extent that it is designed to link directly with job performance participants should be required critically to examine their practice through investigations which stimulate their reflection on evidence collected in the job. Ideally, they should take managerial action in the light of that reflection and gather evidence about the consequences of their action as the basis for further cycles of reflection and action.

7
EVALUATING LEARNING SUPPORT PROGRAMMES

The feedback that evaluation may offer to programme managers and policy-makers is possibly one of the most important factors that contributes to the effectiveness of learning support programmes. Paradoxically, the value of the service to be gained from evaluation is not always perceived. It is quite possible to implement programmes with little or no evaluation, relying upon an act of faith that the programme influences performance in the job, represents an efficient use of scarce resources, and is well received by participants. Such evaluation evidence on learning support activities as we have suggests that this act of faith may not always be justified. Programmes can fail to achieve the outcomes intended by policy-makers and programme managers and they may give rise to unintended and undesirable consequences. If the maximum benefit is to be gained from a given level of investment in learning support, programme managers should seek feedback based upon sound evidence at regular opportunities during all but the shortest programmes and after any programme is completed.

In common with learning support activities, there are usually severe constraints upon the level of resources that may be invested in evaluation. It is also advisable to limit the extent of the evaluation evidence collected both to prevent this activity from becoming overly intrusive and to avoid gathering vast amounts of evidence that evaluators do not have time to analyse. Thus evaluation design is centrally concerned with making effective and unobtrusive use of limited resources to sample and record the judgements of those involved in what happens before, during and after a programme. The aim is to maximize feedback available to programme managers and policy-makers for the benefit of participants.

It is for this reason that we stressed in Chapter 5 that evaluation should be planned as an integral part of learning support programmes and should therefore feature in outline within the initial programme design. Once the initial programme design and accompanying initial evaluation brief are approved by the policy-makers who have overall responsibility for the programme, it is possible to firm up an evaluation brief as a basis for designing the evaluation itself. The examples of programmes described in the previous chapter illustrate how programme designs may valuably include points for the collection of evaluation evidence which should be reflected in the evaluation brief. The present chapter addresses the detailed process of evaluation design for which the evaluation brief is the starting point.

Evidently the scale and complexity of evaluation tasks will vary with the nature of the programme and the resources available for evaluation. At one extreme is the short school based programme consisting of a single activity, where the programme manager is also responsible for evaluation. At the other extreme is the long external programmme, consisting of many activities, where independent evaluators are employed.

General principles of evaluation may apply in all cases:

- The *purposes* of the evaluation suggest the *focus*. For example, where a purpose is to improve the programme, the evaluation will include a focus upon the effectivenes of the activities.
- *Questions* are posed that imply criteria for judging effectiveness within the focus. A question related to the effectiveness of activities might be: 'was the content of the activities relevant to meet participants' needs?' A criterion of effectiveness in this instance is the degree to which the content of activities relates to learning support needs. Implicitly, the assumption about effectiveness against which activities are to be judged is that 'effective activities are directly relevant to participants' needs for learning support'.
- *Evidence* is gathered in order to answer the questions that have been posed, in our example by seeking the views of participants on the relevance of activity content to their perceived needs.
- The evidence is summarized, a process requiring *interpretation*. Participants in the example may vary in their views about relevance of the content of activities to their perceived needs. Although responses may be collated, some interpretation has to be made in categorizing responses and in summarizing the disparate comments in an overall conclusion. Here the summary might be; 'two thirds of the participants stated that the content of activities was of moderate relevance to their needs and one-third stated that it was largely irrelevant'.
- *Conclusions* are drawn that represent answers to the questions. The conclusion in the example might be that the content of activities was generally seen not to be closely relevant to participants' perceived needs.
- Further interpretation is involved in *reporting* these conclusions and making recommendations based on them. In this case a recommendation might be that the content of activities was more specifically targeted in future upon participants' management tasks in school.

However, the size of the programme and the scale of the evaluation will make a difference to the number and complexity of the evaluation management tasks and their links with programme management, to the range of design considerations and to the number of people involved. Equally, there are different approaches to evaluation. The approach described here is built upon advice for organizers of school management training courses monitored during the 1980s by the NDC (Eraut, 1985). An account will be given of the management and design of an independent evaluation of a substantial external programme, so as to cover the range of tasks and considerations that readers are likely to meet. This account will be illustrated in the final part of this chapter by describing an example of such a programme evaluation.

Some parts of the evaluation management process may be condensed for short or school based programmes where, for example the programme manager is responsible for evaluation, or where there is little choice of methods. Certain of the evaluation instruments presented below may be adapted for less comprehensive evaluations. For a very helpful account of evaluation which focuses exclusively upon staff (and management) development activities organized by staff in schools see Oldroyd and Hall (1991b).

Managing evaluation

The process of managing evaluation is dictated in large part by the process of programme management that it serves. These links are shown in Figure 7.1 which incorporates the strategic and detailed activities of programme management outlined in Chapter 5 (and depicted in Figure 5.1) with two additional activities for programme managers. The right hand side of the diagram indicates the main acitivities that fall to evaluators.

The following sequence of activities summarizes the process of managing an evaluation. Evaluators receive the *evaluation brief* which has been drawn up by programme managers after consulting policy-makers (say, a steering committee) and revising the initial programme design in the light of their comments. The initial design includes an outline of the evaluation brief which policy-makers are asked to approve. In order to draw up an *evaluation design,* evaluators must be made familiar with the details of the revised programme design. Once the evaluation design is complete an *action plan* is developed and programme managers are consulted to *facilitate the collection of evidence* for the evaluation. *Implementation* entails gathering and interpreting evidence, leading to conclusions being drawn and recommendations being made. Regular *informal feedback* is given to the programme managers, possibly accompanied by occasional, more formal *interim reports*. These forms of feedback support formative evaluation of the programme, possibly leading to the modification of activities and their sequencing. Liaison may take place between policy-makers and programme managers (and possibly the evaluators), enabling policy-makers to steer the programme in the light of formative evaluation evidence, conclusions and recommendations.

The Process of Programme Management

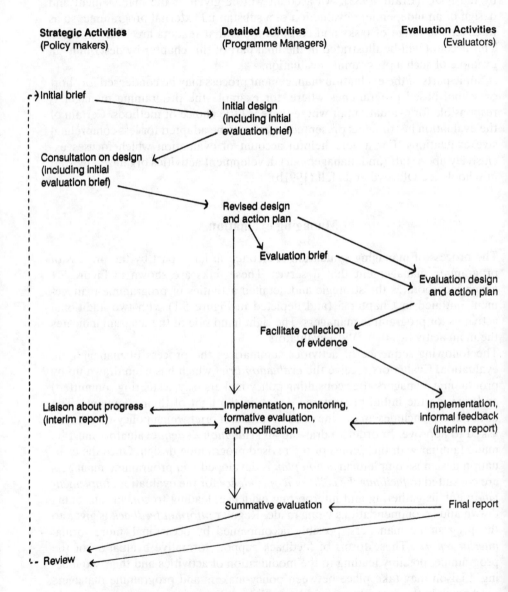

Strategic Activities
(Policy makers)

Detailed Activities
(Programme Managers)

Evaluation Activities
(Evaluators)

Initial brief

Initial design
(including initial
evaluation brief)

Consultation on design
(including initial
evaluation brief)

Revised design
and action plan

Evaluation brief

Evaluation design
and action plan

Facilitate collection
of evidence

Liaison about progress
(interim report)

Implementation, monitoring,
formative evaluation,
and modification

Implementation,
informal feedback
(interim report)

Summative evaluation

Final report

Review

Figure 7.1: The process of managing programme evaluation

Once all evidence is gathered, possibly some months after the programme ends, the evaluators prepare a *final report*, which is presented to the programme managers to support summative evaluation of the quality and impact of the programme. Policy-makers, programme managers and evaluators contribute to a review of the programme, drawing upon the evidence, conclusions and recommendations of the final report.

The evaluation brief

Immediately the programme design is finalized (see Chapter 5) an important task for programme managers is to draw up an evaluation brief and to use it, together with the programme design itself, as a basis for negotiating with prospective evaluators. The aim is to provide evaluators with a clear idea about what is required of them so that they may plan the most effective way of carrying out their brief within the parameters they are set. An evaluation brief may contain the following guidance for evaluators:

- the purposes of the evaluation (e.g. to assess impact on participants' job performance);
- its focus (e.g. upon action in school as a result of programme activities);
- the audience who will receive any form of report (e.g. a programme steering committee);
- major questions to be answered which imply criteria of effectiveness (e.g. what is the impact of particular activities upon participants' managerial performance in school?);
- suggested methods to be used for gathering evidence (e.g. interview, questionnaire);
- the sources of evidence (e.g. participants, trainers, LEA advisers);
- the suggested timing of activities for collecting evidence (e.g. time set aside during the first and final days of a substantial programme);
- the required form of reports (e.g. verbal, full written report, written executive summary);
- deadlines for reporting (e.g. interim report half way through and final report three months after the programme);
- resources available (e.g. total number of days for which evaluators' services are to be contracted, secretarial support).

The more clearly the brief states the focus and outcomes, the easier it is for programme managers to ensure that evaluators provide the service they require. On the other hand, it is advisable not to constrain evaluators by overly detailed specification of the methods that they will employ to answer the key evaluation questions. Figure 7.2 is a form which may be used to specify an evaluation brief.

Title of Programme:

Dates of Programme: *from*   *to*

Purposes of evaluation:

Focus:

Audience for reports:

Key questions to address:

Suggested methods for collecting evidence:

Sources of evidence:

Suggested timing of evidence collection:

Format of reports:

Deadlines for reporting:

Resources available:

Programme manager's name, address and telephone number:

Figure 7.2:   A form for an evaluation brief

Designing an evaluation

The process of design may be summarized as a series of steps whose detail will depend upon the scale of the programme and the resources available for evaluation:

(1) Clarify the main parameters within which the evaluation is to be designed, including its purposes, focus, audiences, reporting requirements, opportunities for collecting evidence, arrangements for protecting confidentiality and the resources available.
(2) Pose questions which will address the stated purposes of the evaluation.
(3) Identify the sources of evidence to answer the evaluation questions.
(4) Select methods of collecting evidence.
(5) Decide upon the sample of programme activities to evaluate and the informants whose views are to be sought.
(6) Identify the points by which any evaluation instruments must be ready for use and (not necessarily at the same time) design instruments.
(7) Decide how evidence will be collated and interpreted.
(8) Clarify the form of reports and their audiences.
(9) Draw up a timetable of all activities entailed in the evaluation.
(10) Consider how the evaluation work may be monitored, evaluated and modified if necessary.

These design steps will be described in order but in reality are likely to be considered together. Evaluators will go back and forth between steps as they work out particular components of the design. For example, designing any evaluation instrument requires consideration of the questions to ask, the sources of evidence, the method of collection, sampling, and the strategy for analysing the evidence gained within the relevant deadline for reporting.

The first step for evaluators is to check the main parameters within which they will have to operate. The purposes, focus and key questions of the evaluation, coupled with the level of resourcing, will influence decisions about methods for collecting evidence and sampling.

Posing questions

Some broad questions may be stated in the evaluation brief. The second step is to identify a set of questions which both fulfil the purposes of the evaluation and are feasible to address within the resources available. Each of these questions implies criteria of effectiveness against which the programme is to be judged. It is a simple matter to think of myriad questions, but equally easy to end up with a large number of piecemeal questions which may fail to reflect the most important criteria of effectiveness. Therefore, the selection of questions is worth careful thought.

Two approaches to the posing of questions will be discussed. The first involves identifying reasonably specific questions and the second is based upon fewer broad questions. Readers will find examples of both types of question in the evaluation instruments included in the latter part of this chapter.

One way to begin is to pre-specify the criteria of effectiveness that relate to each evaluation purpose and its focus. For example, a common purpose is to improve the present and possible future programmes for which an evaluation may focus upon the quality of the learning support provided by the programme and its impact upon participants' job performance. The principles put forward in Chapter 2 on the basis of research, professional knowledge and theory, and the related analysis of learning and effective learning support in Chapter 5, suggest some of the key factors that promote effective programmes.

Let us use the example of a substantial external training course whose stated purpose is to improve participants' job performance. An effective programme may include:

- the prior identification of participants' needs;
- briefing of trainers about these needs;
- selection of participants according to explicit criteria, including those that relate to these needs;
- procedures for informing participants why they are selected;
- means of preparing participants for activities so that the learning support experience builds upon their existing experience;
- articulated aims for each activity which support the stated purpose of the programme;
- briefing of participants about these aims;
- aims which are feasible to achieve within the constraints of the programme;
- the establishment of a learning agreement with participants;
- preparatory and ongoing support for facilitators;
- content of activities that is perceived by participants as relevant to their identified needs;
- methods or processes for supporting learning through activities which are appropriate to facilitate participants' learning;
- a setting which fosters full participation in learning support activities;
- opportunities to plan action in school after activities;
- the provision of follow-up support through activities in school and support from other staff;
- frequent opportunities for formative evaluation by participants;
- the avoidance of stereotypical assumptions based on gender, race, age, sexual orientation or disability;
- the direct outcome that participants' job performance is improved;
- the indirect outcome that the job performance is improved of those adults with and through whom the participants carry out their management tasks;
- the efficient use of resources invested in the programme.

Each of these criteria of effectiveness may be turned into a specific question. For example: 'were the management development needs of participants identified prior to the programme?'. Each question leads to consideration of the sources of relevant evidence, the best time to collect it, and how it may be collected. Since it is possible that the various parties directly involved may disagree about the answer to a question it is crucial to ensure that representatives of all parties are approached for information. Participants' needs may have been identified by programme managers on the basis of their professional experience, for instance, but not checked out with individual participants or not communicated to trainers. In the above example evidence should be sought from participants, programme managers and trainers. This approach leads to quite a large number of fairly specific questions which together cover a spectrum of effectiveness criteria. Each question may form part of the content of instruments for gathering evidence.

An alternative route is to rely upon relatively few broad questions in which several criteria of effectiveness may be implicit, thus covering a range of considerations with each question. Fewer criteria of effectiveness are pre-specified in this approach. A wide coverage question is: 'what are the main strengths and weaknesses of the programme?'. Implicit in this question are several effectiveness criteria that participants may apply, such as relevance to their perceived needs, adequate preparatory work, clear briefing about the aims of activities, efficient and unobtrusive administration, the setting being conducive to learning, the methods being stimulating but unthreatening, or the provision of follow-up support which is helpful. These implicit criteria may be teased out from responses to the question and reflected in the interpretation of evidence collected. This question may also be put to trainers, where it may reveal somewhat different criteria of effectiveness. For example, one criterion may be adequate communication by programme managers to enable activities to be designed to meet participants' needs.

Gathering evidence

The third design step is to identify the sources of evidence. We have indicated above that evidence should be sought from representatives of all parties whose experience and action is implicated in the topic of a question. In a substantial external training programme a set of activities may involve participants, trainers and facilitators. The work of programme managers may have influenced the design and implementation of these activities. Depending upon the availability of the various parties, evidence on a particular question may be sought from each party, if necessary by a different method.

The fourth step is to select methods for gathering evidence. Four in common use are observation, questionnaires, interviews and document collection. Each method has its advantages and disadvantages, summarized in Table 7.1. Selection of methods requires fine judgements to be made on how most effectively to gather the necessary evidence within the constraints at hand. The process of weighing up the advantages against the disadvantages of

Table 7.1: Methods of gathering evidence

Method	Advantages	Disadvantages
Direct observation of learning support activities	Direct experience for evaluators Personal contact with informants Unobtrusive	Relies on evaluators' interpretation Time-consuming Fragmented – samples small parts of programme
Questionnaires – pre-programme (*to aid planning*) – end of activities within programme (*for immediate feedback*) – end of programme (*to assess quality and intended action in school*) – after end of programme (*to assess impact on action in school*)	Easy to administer Easy to collate evidence Can be analysed at any time	Need careful design Impersonal Unpopular with those who have to complete them Time consuming to analyse People may be unwilling to write down what they may be prepared to say Over-emphasizes strong positive or negative responses
Interviews *(formal or informal, individual or group, face to face or telephone)*	Immediate responses Interactive: encourages in depth responses	Time consuming to conduct Can be time-consuming to analyse Requires sensitive and skilful interviewing Can be susceptible to distortion through ill-considered responses
Documents *(e.g programme brochure, letter of acceptance to participants, programme timetable)*	A permanent record Can be analysed at any time Provides an overview of programme	Impersonal Time-consuming to analyse

each method and selecting a balance between them may be influenced by several considerations, including:

- time available for attending activities;
- time available for analysing evidence;
- time available for designing instruments, especially questionnaires;
- the availability of documents;
- the danger of overburdening informants with evidence gathering activities;
- the need for in depth understanding of some issues;
- the need to collect evidence from as large a sample of informants as possible;

- the danger of collecting more evidence than can be analysed;
- the availability of secretarial assistance and support with collating evidence, especially that gathered from questionnaires;
- the timing of interim and final reports;
- the evaluators' experience and expertise with particular methods.

Next come sampling decisions. The fifth step for substantial programmes is to work out which activities will be subject to evidence gathering effort and from whom evidence will be collected. The aim is for the sample to represent the range of types of learning experience within the programme design and, as mentioned above, to include all individuals, or a representative sample, from all the parties concerned when addressing each major evaluation question.

The sixth step is to design any instruments to be used for gathering evidence, or at least to work out when instruments will have to be designed and ready for use. Detailed design issues vary with the method to be used and the evaluation questions to be answered. Evidence may be quantitative (e.g. how many participants found an activity relevant to their perceived needs) or qualitative (e.g. a trainer's opinion of the adequacy of her or his briefing), relatively objective (e.g. the number of participants who attended every activity) or relatively subjective (e.g. which activities were most enjoyed by participants). Evaluation instruments are based upon instruments widely used in research of various kinds. Readers who wish to know more about the detailed design of instruments are suggested to refer to the extensive literature on research and evaluation methods. Useful starting points are Henderson (1978), Herman (1987) and Cohen and Manion (1989).

Analysing evidence and reporting

The seventh step is to decide when and how evidence is to be collated and interpreted. It is very important that analysis is as systematic as the collection of evidence. There should be a clear link from evidence to interpretation, and from interpretation to conclusion and recommendation. Evaluators should aim to be in a position such that, if their conclusions and recommendations are challenged, they can justify any statement in their reports by referring back to the evidence on which it is based. For example, a statement that follow-up support in school from colleagues had been received by only a minority of participants should be directly backed by evidence sought from a large enough sample of participants to justify the assertion that is made. It should also be possible for those who receive the evaluation report to assess the strength of the evidence base for its conclusions and recommendations. In our example evidence may have been collected through a questionnaire. If asked, evaluators should be able to state the proportion of those surveyed who responded to the question. Therefore evaluators have to work out the rules by which evidence is to be categorized and a summary interpretation is to be made of it.

Since any interpretation may be contested, it is equally important that any party whose work is to be subject to critique is given the opportunity to comment upon the interpretation that is made and for this interpretation to be acknowledged in the report. If, for instance, the interpretation of evidence collected from participants asserts that the work of a trainer was perceived by the majority of participants to be irrelevant or unstimulating, the trainer should be informed and invited to comment. Analysis of evidence must be completed in time for a draft of any written report to be commented upon by the various parties, especially programme managers, trainers and facilitators.

The eighth step is to clarify the form and sequence of reporting and the audiences for various reports. Evaluators generally expect to give informal verbal feedback to trainers and programme managers at frequent intervals as part of formative evaluation. Any evaluation is likely to culminate in a final, summative report. Policy-makers' expectations about length, detail, format and audience will influence the time required to compile it. How widely the report will be disseminated and the agreement reached about protecting anonymity and evidence offered in confidence will affect what may be written. Once the report is handed over, evaluators lose control over its use. Evaluators should, perhaps, consider the possibility that the document could subsequently be made public, whatever the original agreement about dissemination.

In the case of substantial programmes spread out over several months, evaluators may be asked to prepare an interim report whose purpose may be both to provide formative feedback on the present programme and to inform the design of any planned repetition of the programme. Where it is offered annually, decisions may have to be made about the design of the next programme before the present one is completed. An interim report can be an important source of information for policy-makers and managers responsible for the subsequent programme.

One of the most important design steps is the ninth: drawing up a timetable of evaluation activities and deadlines. Activities in this context include not only evidence gathering work but also all the arranging that has to precede and follow it. Questionnaires for example, have to be designed, printed, and handed out or sent by post, the responses returned by a given date and analysed in time for reporting. It may be worth avoiding setting too tight a timetable at the outset so that there is room for slippage if unforeseen events occur, such as the postponement of a module of the programme or delay in receiving questionnaire returns.

The final step is to consider how evaluators may monitor and evaluate their work and modify their strategy if necessary. Since evaluation is dependent upon progress with the programme itself, where the programme changes so planned evaluation activities may have to change. In addition, it is important that evaluators maintain a high level of awareness about the impact of their work on the people involved in the programme. If, for example, participants find evaluation interviews overly obtrusive, other methods may have to be tried.

Implementing an evaluation

Careful planning is needed to translate an evaluation design into action. A key consideration for any action plan is to consult programme managers as soon as possible both to ensure that intended activities will mesh with plans for the programme and to enable programme managers to facilitate the gathering of evidence. For example, where individual participants are to be interviewed, a time must be agreed when they will not miss an important input and a venue will be required where they will not be disturbed.

Implementation of the evaluation will require ongoing communication between evaluators and programme managers to administer the various activities for collecting evidence. It is important that participants and any external trainers are informed of the evaluation, that the evaluators are introduced to them, and that their support for the evaluation is sought at the earliest opportunity. Evaluation instruments may have to be designed and printed, evidence will have to be collected and analysed, informal feedback given and formal reports written and presented. The final task for independent evaluators is to present programme managers with the bill!

A design for the evaluation of an external training programme

A short account of the independent evaluation of a substantial external programme is included here to illustrate one approach to the management of an evaluation and some of the considerations that may go into the design of instruments. The programme is fictional but based on real experience. Some of the evaluation instruments employed by the evaluator are included in Appendix One. Readers may wish to refer to these instruments to see in greater detail how design considerations were reflected in their content.

This programme was the first run of what was planned to be an annual training programme for headteachers and deputy headteachers of secondary schools in one LEA. The policy-making group was a steering committee made up of heads and deputies, the programme director and an LEA adviser responsible for management development. The director was a headteacher who had been seconded previously for a term to a higher education institution. During her fellowship there, she had conducted a survey to identify needs among heads and deputies in the LEA and had produced an initial design for the present programme which was intended to respond to the major needs identified. The decision had been taken by the steering committee to appoint freelance trainers who were responsible for delivering the taught component of the programme within the brief set by the steering committee.

The programme was based at the LEA's training institution and consisted of a half-day preparatory meeting and five modules spaced over several months, the first lasting three days and the remainder lasting two. A letter was sent to all secondary heads in the LEA inviting them to attend the programme with one of their deputies and stating that applications would be accepted on a first come, first served basis until the programme was full. The target was twenty-four participants from twelve schools. It was suggested that the deputies who did not attend the programme should be regularly updated and consulted by the head and deputy who did attend on issues arising from the programme which had implications for the school.

An adaptation of action learning sets was planned to run alongside the taught component, the head and deputy from three schools making up each set. Participants from each school were invited at the preparatory meeting to identify an individual or joint management problem connected with their work in school One head in each set was a member of the steering committee for the programme. This person was to act both as the set adviser and as a participant setting an example to others in the set by working on his or her own management problem or one shared with the deputy. Participants were allocated to their set by the programme director and time was allocated during each module for the sets to meet in separate rooms. Set advisers also acted as group facilitators during the sessions led by the trainers.

The purpose of the programme was stated as being 'to improve the management, support and practice of the learning processes in schools', which was broken down into four aims:

- encouraging the analysis of participants' role and skills;
- developing their confidence in using these managerial skills;
- promoting networking within and between institutions;
- promoting effective links with the local community of the school.

The evaluation brief for the programme is included in Figure 7.3.

Its stated purpose was solely concerned with improving this first run of the programme and informing the planning of the next, and so focused upon the quality and impact of the programme. The two key questions directed the evaluator's attention to collecting evidence upon responses to the trainers' input and assessing impact upon participants' job performance. The evaluator was to be accountable to the programme steering committee. An interim report was required by the committee to be presented half-way through the programme in time for decisions to be made about the design of the next programme. In particular, the interim report was to inform the impending decision whether to book the same trainers or to look elsewhere. The evaluator was to be employed for a total of fifteen days, a key parameter affecting the evaluation design.

Designing the evaluation

The design process followed the ten steps outlined above. First, most parameters were clear from the evaluation brief and the programme outline which was supplied to the evaluator. A follow-up telephone conversation with the programme director enabled all relevant points to be checked. For example, the confidentiality arrangements planned for the action learning sets meant that the evaluator would not be able to observe them in action without the permission of the members of each set. The evaluator also sought clarification on

Title of Programme: Secondary School Management Programme 1990-91

Dates of Programme: *from* 26th September 1990 *to* 15th March 1991

Purposes of Evaluation: to improve the present programme and to inform the planning of the programme for 1991-92

Focus: the quality and impact of the training activities within the programme

Audience for reports: members of Programme Steering Committee

Key questions to address: 1.   How far does the trainer's input meet participants' needs?

                                  2.   What is the impact of the programme on participants' managerial practice in school?

Suggested methods for
collecting evidence: observation, limited interviewing, questionnaire, document collection

Sources of evidence: participants, trainers, programme director

Suggested timing of
evidence collection: It would be convenient for contact with participants to take place on final day of each module. Interviews could be arranged with participants after the programme is over.

Format of reports: Verbal interim report to the Steering Committee focusing on the key questions and improving the design of next year's programme.

Deadlines for reporting: Interim report ready for presentation by 15th January 1991
                          Final report ready for presentation by 15th July 1991

Resources available: evaluator's fee for 15 days' work. LEA will arrange interviews after the programme is over and will send out questionnaires.

(Name, address and phone number of programme director)

Figure 7.3:   Evaluation brief for the secondary school management programme confidentiality and the release of evidence. It was agreed that any evidence collected would be treated as 'on the record' unless specifically labelled as confidential. When in doubt, the evaluator would check with those concerned. The reports would not identify participants but would emphasize general issues arising in relation to the purpose of the evaluation. The trainers, programme director and LEA adviser, who were readily identifiable, would be informed about the content of the interim report and shown a draft of the final report before they were presented. Their comments would be incorporated into the reports.

Second, evaluation questions were derived by listing effectiveness criteria relating to the two key questions, drawing upon the evaluator's experience and knowledge of research into external training programmes. The list was similar to the illustration given earlier in this chapter. From this list a bank of questions was created for use in the evaluation instruments.

The second key question, for example, implied that, if the programme was effective, it would meet its purpose of leading to improved job performance on the part of participants. A major evaluation question was: 'what, if any, impact has the programme had upon participants' work as managers in school?'. This question could be broken down into more detailed questions such as: 'with which colleagues, if any, have participants discussed the initiation of changes in school as a result of the programme?', and 'what, if any, changes in school have participants actually initiated as a result of the programme?'.

The evaluator was aware of research evidence that follow-up support is likely to foster action to improve performance after an external training experience. The programme outline suggested that participants from the same school would be encouraged to support each other in school. A related question was therefore: 'what, if any, follow-up support did each participant receive from her or his colleague from the same school who also attended the programme?'.

Third, the evaluator determined that evidence would need to be collected from individuals or representatives of groups directly involved in the activities which made up the programme. These people were participants, participants acting as set advisers and group facilitators, trainers, the programme director and the LEA adviser who represented the interest of the LEA.

Fourth, the limit upon the number of days which the evaluator could spend meant that a balance of methods would offer the best chance of sampling as wide a range of activities and as many people's views as possible. Consequently the methods selected were questionnaires, formal interviews and shorter informal interviews, observation and document collection.

Fifth, as not all activities could be sampled directly, the evaluator decided to collect some evidence from participants at the end of each module, to visit the programme at the end of the first, third and final modules, and sample the views of participants about six weeks after the end of the programme. A mixture of methods would be used to gather evidence from all participants on some occasions and from a sample on others.

Sixth, the instruments for gathering evidence were designed to answer the evaluation questions at the appropriate point in the evaluation. For instance, the initial questionnaire for participants covered the processes of needs identification, selection of participants, and preparation for the first module. The final questionnaire focused upon action in school as a result of participation in the programme.

Seventh, the timetable of evidence gathering was worked out to allow time for collating by hand and for analysis to be completed prior to the preparation of the interim and final reports. Where possible, responses were quantified and tables prepared showing, for example, how many respondents to a questionnaire gave a particular answer to a question.

Eighth, the evaluator checked the approximate length of the verbal input required for the interim report and the maximum length of the final written report. The topics that the evaluator expected to be covered in the interim and final reports were mapped out as a series of headings.

Ninth, a timetable of evaluation activities was drawn up which indicated when particular methods were to be employed, instruments were to be ready for use, evidence analysed and reports compiled. The evaluator worked to this timetable in planning when to communicate with various parties to arrange for each phase of evidence collection as the evaluation proceeded.

Finally, questions about the intrusiveness and effectiveness of the evaluation were included in certain evaluation instruments and the evaluator planned to check with the trainers and programme director during each visit. The perceptions of members of the steering committee about the value of the interim report were to be checked at the meeting when it was presented.

The considerations that featured in the design of the evaluation are reflected in the timetable of evaluation activities and their links with the structure and sequencing of the programme illustrated in Table 7.2. A number in brackets beside an evaluation activity indicates that the relevant instrument is included or summarized in Appendix One in the order in which they were used in the evaluation.

Readers may wish to bear in mind the following issues in examining the evaluation instruments:

- every item within an instrument relates to one of the evaluation questions derived from the list of effectiveness criteria, which are derived in turn from the purpose and focus of the evaluation indicated in the brief;
- the activity observation schedule gives prompts to direct the attention of the evaluator towards behaviour which relates to the evaluation questions;
- some evaluation questions appear in the relevant instrument for different informants both to ensure that the views of all parties are sought and to highlight any disjunction between experiences;
- questionnaires include closed questions or statements where respondents judge which pre-specified category best fits their response. These items are very easily quantified. Most of these closed questions are backed by more open questions or statements giving respondents more scope to express their views. The evaluator will have to work out rules for categorizing these

Table 7.2: **Link between programme structure and evaluation**

Time	Programme structure	Evaluation
		• Briefing, design • Documents received
	Preparatory meeting (1 day)	
		• Questionnaire sent to LEA adviser (*No 1*)
	Module 1 (3 days)	• Observation – half day, documents collected (*No. 2*) • Interviews: trainer; director (*No. 3*) • Initial questionnaire: participants (*No. 4*) • Informal feedback given
		• Analysis of evidence
	Module 2 (2 days)	• Participant's activity evaluation sheet (*No. 5*)
	Module 3 (2 days)	• Observation – half day, documents collected • Informal interviews: sample of participants; trainer; set advisers; director • mid-programme questionnaire: participants (*No. 6*) • Informal feedback given • Analysis of evidence
		• Interim verbal report given to Steering Committee
	Module 4 (2 days)	• Participants' activity evaluation sheet
		• Analysis of evidence
	Module 5 (2 days)	• Observation – half day, documents collected • Informal interviews: sample of participants; trainer; set advisers; director • Informal feedback given
		• Final questionnaire; participants (*No. 7*) • Interviews: sample of participants, set advisers (*No. 8*) • Analysis of evidence • Draft written report checked with trainer; director • Final written report presented to Steering Committee

The numbers in brackets indicate that the relevant instrument is included in the Appendix.

responses in order to provide a summary of the commonest responses and their full range;
- the activity evaluation sheets are used for a single activity occupying one or more sessions. The trainers who lead this activity insert the activity aims and indicate which aims are covered by each session;
- there is some overlap between the evaluation questions covered in the three questionnaires for participants, although each questionnaire has a different primary focus. Certain issues arise at a single point in a programme, for example the selection process and experience of the preparatory day. Others, such as preparation for each module, occur throughout the programme, while issues like impact upon job performance arise during and after the programme.

The final report

Policy-makers indicated to the evaluator that they wanted the final report to be brief – no more than a few pages. It should include neither the raw evidence collected nor the tables used for analysis. However, the evaluator would be expected to be in a position to give summary information if asked to do so when the report was presented. Accordingly, he brought the tables to the steering committee meeting and referred to them in response to questions from members wishing to know the grounds for particular conclusions or recommendations in the report. The evaluator wrote the report under four headings.

(1) A summary of the evaluation brief.
(2) A summary of the evaluation strategy by which the evaluator responded to the brief.
(3) An account of the main findings under three sub-headings linked to the two key questions that the evaluator was asked to address:
  - How far does the trainers' input meet participants' needs?
  - Other issues connected with the programme.
  - What was the impact of the programme on participants' managerial practice in school?
(4) Recommendations to the steering group.

The draft report was sent to the trainers for comment and their response incorporated and indicated in the text. Subsequently the steering committee decided to send a copy of the report to the chief education officer as part of the agreement to give an account of the programme for which the committee had been responsible, and to circulate it to participants. The document thus came to serve the purpose of accountability in addition to the purpose of programme improvement for which the evaluation had originally been commissioned.

8

MAKING SCHOOL-CENTRED MANAGEMENT TRAINING WORK

Learning support within management development

Throughout this handbook it has been stressed that the ever increasing range of learning support activities and programmes for senior staff in schools has much to offer in promoting improvement in school management. We have also emphasized that this potential will not be realized unless programmes centre upon the school by linking with participants' job experience and managerial tasks. In this sense, learning support is aimed at *manager* development.

However, resources for learning support will inevitably be limited if support activities are not to get in the way of the job itself, a conclusion supported by the model of management development adopted by the Task Force. The basis of management development is viewed as the effort that all school managers must make to learn through doing the job, within a favourable environment which is a key responsibility of headteachers to create and maintain. Equally, it seems unlikely that sufficient central or local government funds will be made available to meet all possible learning needs through support activities, especially at a time of major reform. Therefore, learning support must be directed at high priority individual, group and school wide needs arising from the individual and joint tasks that promote effective school management for the sake of effective education of pupils. Training and other forms of learning support which centre on the school should thus be aimed at *management* development, rather than being concerned solely with the individuals through whose corporate efforts school management is improved.

It has been argued at several points that the deeply value laden nature of management should be more widely acknowledged. The long-term dangers should be considered of failure to support managers in learning to make more fully informed professional judgements in the light of articulated and justified beliefs and values. Effective learning support is not simply about improving technical capability; it is also *educational* in the sense of promoting critical understanding and awareness as a platform from which more fully informed judgements may be made. Learning support should therefore include a focus upon *why* management tasks should or should not be performed as well as a focus upon the performance itself. Doing wrong things effectively may be worse for pupils' education in the long run than doing right things ineffectively. We have followed the argument through that learning support must begin and end with participants' job performance and therefore should meet their needs related to their present or future management tasks. All five components of learning support – diagnosis, developing critical understanding, provision of practical information, practising skills and integration into a skilful performance – have a major contribution to make to justifiable, not merely technically efficient, management in schools.

The close articulation between learning needs and learning support necessary for learning support to centre on the school implies a considerable degree of co-ordination within and between levels of the education service. A range of needs may be identified in any school, in schools across an LEA or a region, or in schools throughout the country. An extensive range of learning support programmes may be identified that are capable of contributing to meeting these needs. Such learning support may be developed by members of a multiplicity of organizations, whether staff in a school or group of schools, in a single LEA or regional group, or trainers in a single higher education institution or consortium, and from a wide assortment of other bases.

Identifying needs of those with and aspiring towards management responsibility in schools, matching needs with learning support and evaluating the effect of these activities is a process that has to be managed at school level. LEAs are held responsible by central government for the professional development of teaching staff in schools. They provide some of the funds for management development and programmes of learning support. The process of managing management development in school must articulate with the process of co-ordinating the identification of management development needs in schools across the LEA, providing a range of substantial learning support programmes and resources for schools to develop their own, and evaluating learning support in the LEA. As the Task Force report emphasizes, LEAs may plan some of their provision as a regional consortium so as to benefit from economies of scale. Regional provision entails continual liaison between such LEAs to make sure that common needs are identified, learning support programmes are designed and implemented, and the initiative is evaluated to check how far these needs have been met.

Management development for schools is a central government priority which attracts considerable funding as it is perceived as an important means of promoting the implementation of the government's reform programme. LEAs are required to demonstrate that they are adopting a co-ordinated approach to provision for which this funding is used. LEAs and, increasingly, schools are able to purchase learning support programmes from a variety of institutions and independent consultants who provide training. Close liaison is required between LEAs or schools and these providers to ensure that they are fully informed about the needs that their programmes are to be designed to meet and the purchasing power that is likely to be available. Evaluation of these programmes is a responsibility that falls both to providers and their clients.

Effective external learning support programmes, whether originating with LEAs or other providers, help bridge the gap between learning support and participants' job performance. Building such a bridge requires liaison between staff in school and the providers. Learning support activities should be designed to promote integration of what has been learned through the support activity into skilful job performance and to foster a climate favourable to experimentation in the job.

The way forward or backward?

The evidence of research and professional experience suggests three prescriptions for improving the effectiveness of learning support which centres upon the school. Firstly, the design of activities and programmes should follow what is known from research, professional knowledge and theory about effective support for the process of learning for managerial performance – the main focus of this handbook. Secondly, these activities and programmes should be evaluated as rigorously as possible to ensure that they really produce the goods and, if not, to indicate where improvements may be made. Thirdly, considerable effort is needed to increase the degree of co-ordination of school management development nationally, regionally and locally (the focus of other publications in this series).

Despite increasing acknowledgement in recent years of the role effective management may play in promoting effective schools, the conditions in this country for management development are in some ways less favourable than in the late 1980s, as was hinted in Chapter 1. Learning support programmes that directly promote integration of learning into an individual's job performance through observation and feedback by others tend to be labour intensive. Those with a strong emphasis on education for critical understanding also tend to be costly where the opportunity is given for the periods of full-time study that are so important for sustained reflection and in depth study.

The steady increase in funding from central government since the early 1980s, which has been widely used to meet long-term management development needs, has become skewed towards the short-term goals of managing government reforms. The heavy demand for practical information to be given to senior staff throughout the country over a very short period has resulted in a tendency to sacrifice depth of support for breadth of cover. As we have seen, short workshops or distance learning are both valuable but cannot provide much direct support for the vital process of integration into job performance. At a time when learning support is critical for the successful implementation of central government reforms, resource constraints may put a squeeze on the kind of support that could really help to make the necessary impact on performance in the job.

The high priority to deliver the maximum amount of training to the greatest possible number may also limit the use of thorough evaluation that assesses impact. It is difficult and relatively expensive, whereas superficial evaluation of programme quality is straightforward and much cheaper to carry out. This trend is reinforced by central government's approach to learning support, leaving the customers largely to decide its quality by voting with their feet. If trainers do not give the customers satisfaction, they do not get asked back. However, when there is such a demand for their services, there are always plenty of new customers to go round.

The belief of ministers that a national education service can be run more effectively on the lines of successful companies, with institutions competing in the marketplace, has led to a series of changes for the various partners in the service. Since 1987, providers of management training from higher education and elsewhere have been competing for the custom of LEAs and schools; with the advent of LMS, schools are placed in competition with each other for the custom of parents; LEAs are under pressure to devolve a high proportion of funds for in-service training to schools so that the latter may decide whether or not to purchase LEA provision. Competition militates against the willingness to collaborate that is a precondition of close co-ordination between institutions at the same and different levels. It remains to be seen how far deep rooted professional values that favour collaboration rather than competition will enable the various partners to continue to work together as their roles are changed at the hand of central government ministers. However, there appears still to be plenty of room to manoeuvre to build upon present practice of learning support for managers in schools by making incremental changes. McMahon and Bolam (1990a) suggest that experiments or projects should be developed alongside the maintenance of existing work, rather than radical, sweeping innovation.

Hopefully, this handbook may have provided some useful, though inevitably limited, learning support for readers who are responsible for developing programmes for senior staff in schools and who are interested in experimentation. Chapter 1 was intended to promote diagnosis of the need to make improvements in learning support. Chapter 2 was designed to stimulate the development of critical understanding, drawing upon research, professional knowledge and theory, and to offer some general principles for practice. Chapters 3 and 4 gave practical information about a range of activities and programmes, with some guidance about their potential and limitations according to the model of learning for managerial performance developed earlier. Chapters 5 to 7 offered general principles and some practical tips on the design of programmes and their evaluation. Readers were encouraged to develop their analytical skills by engaging in the tasks of designing learning support programmes. Direct support could not be offered either for the learning of skills or for the integration of what may have been gleaned from the book into a skilful performance as a designer of learning support programmes and their evaluation. Doubtless, in parallel with most

managers, the transition from practical ideas for changing to improved performance in offering learning support programmes will be learned without support
through a problem solving approach to the tasks of design, implementation and
evaluation. *Bon voyage!*

References

Acheson, K. A. and Gall, M. D. (1980) *Techniques in the Clinical Supervision of Teachers*, Longman, London.

Adair, J. (1979) *Action Centred Leadership*, Gower, Aldershot.

Adair, J. (1984) *The Skills of Leadership*, Gower, Aldershot.

Argyris, C. and Schon, D. (1974) *Theory in Practice: Increasing Professional Effectiveness*, Jossey-Bass, London.

Bailey, A. J. (1987) *Support for School Management*, Croom Helm, London.

Ballinger, E. (1984) Management development outside education: some implications for the NDC. Internal working paper, National Development Centre for School Management Training, Bristol.

Bank, J. (1985) *Outdoor Development for Managers*, Gower, Aldershot.

Barnett, B. (1987) Peer-assisted leadership: peer observation and feedback as catalysts for professional growth, in J. Murphy and P. Hallinger (eds.) op. cit.

Barnett, B. *et al* (1984a) *Elementary Principals' Yellow Pages*, Far West Laboratory for Educational Research and Development, San Francisco, Calif.

Barnett, B. *et al* (1984b) *Secondary Principals' Yellow Pages*, Far West Laboratory for Educational Research and Development, San Francisco, California.

Barnett, B., Lee, G. and Mueller, F. (undated) *Peer-Assisted Leadership: A Manual for Trainers*, Far West Laboratory for Educational Research and Development, San Francisco, California.

Beck, T. and Kelly, M. (1989) Using consultancy to help train managers in education, *British Journal of In-Service Education*, Vol. 15, no. 1, pp. 19–24.

Beeby, M. and Rathborn, S. (1983) Development training – using the outdoors in management development, *Management Education and Development*, Vol. 14, no 3, pp. 170–81.

Belbin, R. N. (1981) *Management Teams: Why they Succeed or Fail*, Heinemann, London.

Bell, J., Bush, T., Fox, A., Goodey, J. and Goulding, S. (eds.) (1984) *Conducting Small-Scale Investigations in Educational Management*, Paul Chapman, London.

Binsted, D. and Hodgson, V. (1984) Open and distance learning in management education and training: a positional paper. Occasional Paper. Centre for the Study of Management Learning, University of Lancaster.

Bolam, R. (1982a) *Strategies for School Improvement*. Report for the Organization for Economic Co-operation and Development. University of Bristol.

Bolam, R. (1982b) *School Focused In-Service Training*, Heinemann, London.

Bolam, R. (1988) What is effective INSET?, in NFER (ed.) *Professional Development and INSET: Proceedings of the 1987 NFER Members Conference,* NFER, Slough.

Bolam, R. (1989) Implementing multiple change: some implications for management training, *NUT Education Review,* Vol. 3, no. 1, pp. 6–11.

Bolam, R. (1990) Recent developments in England and Wales, in B. Joyce (ed.) *Changing School Culture through Staff Development,* Association for Supervision and Curriculum Development, Virginia.

Boydell, T. and Pedler, M. (1978) *A Manager's Guide to Self Development,* Gower, Aldershot.

Briault, E. and West, N. (1990) *Primary School Management: Learning from Experience,* NFER-Nelson, Windsor.

Brown, S. and Earley, P. (1990) *Enabling Teachers to Undertake In-Service Education and Training:* A Report for the DES, NFER Slough.

Buckley, J. (1985) *The Training of Secondary School Heads in Western Europe,* NFER-Nelson for the Council of Europe, Windsor.

Buckley, J. and Styan, D. (1988) *Managing for Learning,* Macmillan Education, London.

Buckley, J., Styan, D. and Taylor, J. (1990) *Macmillan School Management Project: Training Materials for Primary Schools,* Macmillan Education, London.

Burgoyne, J. and Stuart, R. (1977) Implicit learning theories as determinants of the effect of management development programmes, *Personnel Review,* Vol. 6, no. 2, pp. 5–14.

Burton, K. (1989) Bringing about gender equality of opportunity in a special school, in P. Lomax (ed.) op. cit.

Casey, D. (1983) The role of the set adviser, in M. Pedler (ed.) op. cit.

Coffey, J. (1977) Open learning opportunities for mature students, in T. C. Davies (ed.), *Open Learning Systems for Mature Students,* Council for Educational Technology Working Paper 14. CET, London.

Cohen, L. and Manion, L. (1989) *Research Methods in Education* (3rd edn), Routledge, London.

Collinson, B. S. and Dunlap, S. F. (1978) Nominal group technique: a process for in-service and staff work, *School Counsellor,* Vol. 26, no. 1, pp. 18–25.

Critchley, B. and Casey, D. (1984) Second thoughts on team building, *Management Education and Development,* Vol. 15, no. 2, pp. 163–75.

Dalin, P. and Rust, V. (1983) *Can Schools Learn?* NFER-Nelson, Windsor.

Davies, J. and Easterby-Smith, M. (1984) Learning and development from managerial work experiences, *Journal of Management Studies,* Vol. 21, no. 2, pp. 169–85

Day, C. and Baskett, H. K. (1982) Discrepancies between intentions and practice: re-examining some basic assumptions about adult and continuing professional education, *International Journal of Lifelong Education,* Vol. 1, no. 2, pp. 143–55.

Day, C., Whitaker, P. and Johnston, D. (1990) *Managing Primary Schools in the 1990s: A Professional Development Approach* (2nd edn), Paul Chapman, London.

Department of Education and Science (1989) *LEA Training Grants Scheme 1989–90: Summary of LEA Responses to DES Questionnaire on INSET Management,* DES, London.

Department of Education and Science (1990) *Developing School Management: The Way Forward.* Report of the School Management Task Force, HMSO, London.

Dunham, J. (1984) *Stress in Teaching,* Croom Helm, London.

Dwyer, D. (1985) Contextual antecedents of instructional leadership, *The Urban Review,* Vol. 17, no. 3, pp. 166–88.

Eraut, M. (1985) *Evaluation of Management Courses: Advice for Course Organisers,* National Development Centre for School Management Training, Bristol.

Eraut, M. (1988) Learning about management: the role of the management course, in C. Poster and C. Day (eds.) op. cit.

Eraut, M., Pennycuick, D. and Radnor, H. (1988) *Local Evaluation of Inset: A Metaevaluation of TRIST Evaluations,* National Development Centre for School

Management Training for the Manpower Services Commission, Bristol.

Esp, D. (1983) Training approaches in various European countries – an overview, in S. Hegarty (ed.) *Training for Management in Schools*, NFER-Nelson for the Council of Europe, Windsor.

Fox, W. M. (1989) The improved nominal group technique (NGT), *Journal of Management Development*, Vol. 8, no. 1, pp. 20–7.

Francis, D. and Woodcock, M. (1982) *50 Activities for Self-Development*, Gower, Aldershot.

Fullan, M. (1991) *The New Meaning of Educational Change*, Cassell, London.

Fullan, M., Miles, M. and Taylor, G. (1980) Organization development in schools: the state of the art, *Review of Educational Research*, Vol. 50, no. 1, pp. 121–84.

Further Education Unit (1989) An evaluation of quality circles in colleges of FE. Planning and implementing post-14 staff development project bulletin no. 7. Further Education Unit, London.

Glatter, R. (1972) *Management Development for the Education Profession*, Harrap, London.

Goldhammer, R. (1969) *Clinical Supervision: Special Methods for the Supervision of Teachers*, Holt, Rinehart & Winston, London.

Goulding, S., Bush, T., Fox, A., Goodey, J. and Bell, J. (eds.) (1984) *Case Studies in Educational Management*, Paul Chapman, London.

Gray, H. L. (ed.) (1988) *Management Consultancy in Schools*, Cassell, London.

Griffin, R. and Cashin, W. (1989) The lecture and discussion method for management education: pros and cons, *Journal of Management Development*, vol. 8, no. 3, pp. 25–32.

Hall, V. (1988) Networks and networking: a working paper. Internal working paper. National Development Centre for School Management Training, Bristol.

Hall, V. and Oldroyd, D. (1990) *Management Self-Development for Staff in Secondary Schools*, National Development Centre for Educational Management and Policy, Bristol.

Hall, V. and Wallace, M. (1991) *Management Self-Development for Staff in Primary Schools*, National Development Centre for Educational Management and Policy, Bristol.

Harries, J. M. (1983) Developing the set adviser, in M. Pedler (ed.) op. cit.

Henderson, E. (1978) *The Evaluation of In-Service Teacher Training*, Croom Helm, London.

Henderson, E. (1979) School focused in-service education and training, *British Journal of Teacher Education*, vol. 5, no. 1, pp. 17–26.

Her Majesty's Inspectorate (1989) *The Implementation of the Local Education Authority Training Grant Scheme (LEATGS): Report on First Year of the Scheme*, Report by HM Inspectors, DES, London.

Herman, J. (ed.) (1987) *The Program Evaluation Kit,* 9 vols. (2nd edn), Sage, London.

Honey, P. and Mumford, A. (1982) *A Manual of Learning Styles*, Peter Honey, Maidenhead.

Honey, P. and Mumford, A. (1983) *Using Your Learning Styles*, Peter Honey, Maidenhead.

House of Commons (1986) *Third Report from the Education, Science and Arts Committee, Session 1985–86: Achievement in Primary Schools, Volume 1*, HMSO, London.

Huczynski, A. (1983) *An Encyclopedia of Management Development Methods*, Gower, Aldershot.

Huczynski, A. and Lewis, J. (1980) An empirical study into the learning transfer process in management training, *Journal of Management Studies*, May, pp. 227–41.

Hughes, M. Carter, J. and Fidler, B. (1981) *Professional Development Provision for Senior Staff in Schools and Colleges*. Research project final report. University of Birmingham.

IMC (1988) Master of Business Administration (Education). Publicity leaflet. International Management Centres, Buckingham.

Joyce, B. and Showers, B. (1980) Improving in-service training: the messages of research, *Educational Leadership*, February, pp. 379–85.

Joyce, B. and Showers, B. (1988) *Student Achievement through Staff Development*, Longman, London.

Kable, J. (1989) Management development through action learning, *Journal of Management Development*, Vol. 8, no. 2, pp. 77–80.

Knowles, M. (1984) *Andragogy in Action: Applying Modern Principles of Adult Learning*, Jossey-Bass, London.

Kolb, D. (1976) *The Learning Style Inventory: Technical Manual*, McBer, Boston, Massachussetts.

Kolb, D. (1984) *Experiential Learning*, Prentice Hall, London.

Kubr, M. (ed.) (1976) *Management Consulting: A Guide to the Profession*, International Labour Office, Geneva.

Lacey, J. D. and Licht, N. C. (1980) Culminating experience: a tool for management training, *Training and Development Journal*, Vol. 34, no. 3, pp. 88–90.

Lavalle, M. and Keith, D. (1988) Internal organization development consultancy in a local education authority, in H. L. Gray (ed.) op. cit.

Leithwood, K. and Montgomery, D. (1986) *The Principal Profile*, OISE Press, Toronto.

Leithwood, K. and Steger, M. (1989) Expertise in principals' problem solving, *Educational Administration Quarterly*, Vol. 25, no. 2, pp. 126–61.

Lewis, L. (ed.) (1986) *Experiential and Simulation Techniques for Adults*, Jossey-Bass, London.

Local Government Training Board (1984) *The Effective Manager: A Resource Handbook*, LGTB, Luton.

Lomax, P. (ed.) (1989) *The Management of Change*, Multilingual Matters, Clevedon.

Louis, K. S. and Miles, M. (1990) *Improving the Urban High School: What Works and Why*, Teachers College Press, New York.

Lyons, G., Stenning, R. and McQueeney, J. (1986) Managing Staff in Schools: Training Materials, Hutchinson, London.

McMahon, A. (1991) *Action Research for School Management Development*, National Development Centre for Educational Management and Policy, Bristol.

McMahon, A. and Bolam, R. (1990a) *School Management Development and Educational Reform: A Handbook for LEAs*, (2nd edn.), Paul Chapman, London.

McMahon, A. and Bolam, R. (1990b) *Management Development and Educational Reform: A Handbook for Primary Schools*, Paul Chapman, London.

McMahon, A. and Bolam, R. (1990c) *Management Development and Educational Reform: A Handbook for Secondary Schools*, Paul Chapman, London.

McNiff, J. (1988) *Action Research: Principles and Practice*, Macmillan Education, Basingstoke.

Megginson, D. and Boydell, T. (1979) *A Manager's Guide to Coaching*, BACIE, London.

Mortimore, P., Sammons, P., Stoll, L., Lewis, D. and Ecob, R. (1988) *School Matters: The Junior Years*, Open Books, Wells.

Mountford, J. (1988) The role of critical friends in school evaluation, *School Organization*, Vol. 8, no. 3, pp. 255–60.

Mumford, A. (1980) *Making Experience Pay*, McGraw-Hill, London.

Mumford, A. (ed.) (1984) *Insights in Action Learning*, MCB University Press, Bradford.

Murphy, J. and Hallinger, P. (1987) *Approaches to Administrative Training in Education*, State University of New York Press, Albany, New York.

Oakeshott, M. (1962) *Rationalism in Politics and Other Essays*, Methuen, London.

Oakeshott, M. (1967) Learning and Teaching, in R. S. Peters (ed.) *The Concept of Education*, Routledge & Kegan Paul, London.

Oldroyd, D. and Hall, V. (1991a) *Managing Staff Development: A Handbook for Secondary Schools*, Paul Chapman, London.

Oldroyd, D. and Hall. V. (1991b) *Management Self Development for Staff in Secondary Schools: Action Research*, National Development Centre for Educational Management and Policy, Bristol.

Paisey, A. (1984) *School Management: A Case Approach*, Paul Chapman, London.

Pearce, D. (1983) Getting started: an action manual, in M. Pedler (ed.) op. cit.

Pedler, M. (ed.) (1983) *Action Learning in Practice*, Gower, Aldershot.

Pedler, M., Burgoyne, J. and Boydell, T. (1978) *A Manager's Guide to Self-Development*, McGraw-Hill, Maidenhead.

Pike, J. (1983) Action learning on an academic course, in M. Pedler (ed.) op. cit.

Pitner, N. (1987) Principles of quality staff development: lessons for administrator training, in J. Murphy and P. Hallinger (eds.) op. cit.

Polanyi, M. and Prosch, H. (1975) *Meaning*, University of Chicago Press.

Poster, C. and Day, C. (1988) *Partnership in Education Management*, Routledge, London.

Preedy, M. (1988) Partnership at a distance, in C. Poster and C. Day (eds.) op. cit.

Rackham, N. and Morgan, T. (1977) *Behaviour Analysis in Training*, McGraw-Hill, London.

Reddy, M. (1985) Counselling in organizations, *Training Officer*, Vol. 2, no. 8, pp.236–9.

Reid, W. A. (1978), *Thinking about the Curriculum*, Routledge & Kegan Paul, London.

Revans, R. (1972) Action learning – a management development programme, *Personnel Review*, Vol. 1, no. 4.

Revans, R. (1982) *The Origins and Growth of Action Learning*, Chartwell Bratt, Bromley.

Robson, M. (ed.) (1984) *Quality Circles in Action*, Gower, Aldershot.

Rodwell, S. (1986) *Educational Administrator Training Methods: A Guide*, University of London Institute of Education.

Rudduck, J. (1981) *Making the Most of the Short In-Service Course*, Schools Council Working Paper No. 71. Methuen, London.

Rutter, M., Maugham, B., Mortimore, P., Ouston, J. and Smith, A. (1979) *Fifteen Thousand Hours: Secondary Schools and their Effects on Children*, Open Books, London.

Schmuck, D. (1982) Organization development for the 1980s, in H. L. Gray (ed.) *The Management of Educational Institutions*, Falmer Press, Lewes.

Schmuck, D. and Runkel, P. (1985) *The Handbook of Organization Development in Schools*, (3rd edn.) Mayfield, London.

Schon, D. (1983) *The Reflective Practitioner*, Basic Books, New York.

Schon, D. (1987) *Educating the Reflective Practitioner*, Jossey-Bass, London.

Scottish Education Department (1989) *Effective Primary Schools*, HMSO, London.

Showers, B. (1985) Teachers coaching teachers, *Educational Leadership,* vol. 42, no. 7, pp. 43–9.

Simon, H. (1989) Making management decisions: the role of intuition and emotion, in W. H. Agor (ed.) *Intuition in Organizations*, Sage, London.

Smith, K. and Phipson, G. (1982) Exchanging jobs, in R. Bolam (ed.) op. cit.

Stuart, R. (1978) Contracting to learn, *Management Education and Development*, Vol. 7, no. 5, pp. 43–65.

Stuart, R. (1983) Training and development: a natural everyday activity, *Management Education and Development*, Vol. 14, no. 3.

Stuart, R. and Binsted, D. (1981) The transfer of learning: designing reality into management learning events, in B. Nixon, (ed.) *New Approaches to Management Development*, Gower, Farnborough.

Taylor, C. (1977) Shadowing: the creative approach to supervisory training, *Management*, Vol. 24, no. 8, pp. 14–15.

Taylor, J. L. and Walford, R. (1978) *Learning and the Simulation Game*, Open University Press, Milton Keynes.

Thorpe, R. (1988) An MSc by action learning: management development initiative by higher degree, *Management Education and Development*, Vol. 19, no. 1, pp. 68–78.

Wallace, M. (1985) Promoting careers through management development, *Education 3–13*, Vol. 13, no. 2, pp. 12–16.

Wallace, M. (1986a) *A Directory of School Management Development Activities and Resources*, National Development Centre for School Management Training, Bristol.

Wallace, M. (1986b) Training and learning – a missing link? *British Journal of In-Service Education*, Vol. 12, no. 2, pp. 68–72.

Wallace, M. (1986c) Towards an action research approach to educational management. Unpublished Ph.D. thesis, University of East Anglia.

Wallace, M. (1987a) A historical review of action research: some implications for the education of teachers in their managerial role, *Journal of Education for Teaching*, Vol. 13, no. 2, pp. 97–115.

Wallace, M. (1987b) Principals' centres: a transferable innovation? *School Organization*, Vol. 7, no. 3, pp. 287–95.

Wallace, M. (1988) *Improving School Management Training: Towards a New Partnership*, National Development Centre for School Management Training, Bristol.

Wallace, M. (1990a) Can action learning live up to its reputation? *Management Education and Development*, Vol. 21, no. 2, pp. 89–103.

Wallace, M. (1990b) *Managing In-Service Training in Primary Schools*, National Development Centre for School Management Training, Bristol.

Wallace, M. (1991) Flexible planning: a key to the management of multiple innovations, *Educational Management and Administration*, vol. 19, no. 3, pp. 180–92.

Wallace, M. Bailey, J. and Kirk, P. (1988) *Action Learning: Practice and Potential in School Management Development*, National Development Centre for School Management Training, Bristol.

Wallace, M. and Hall, V. (1989), Management development and training for schools in England and Wales: an overview, *Educational Management and Administration*, Vol. 17, no. 4, pp. 163–75.

Warwick, D. (1975) *School Based In-Service Training*, Oliver & Boyd, Edinburgh.

West, N. (1987) Acting headship in the primary school – some management issues, *Education 3–13*, March, Vol. 15, part 1, p. 51–6.

Woodcock, M. (1979) *Team Development Manual,* Gower, Aldershot.

Woodcock, M. and Francis, D. (1979) *The Unblocked Manager: A Practical Guide to Sel-Development*, Gower, Aldershot.

Woodcock, M. and Francis, D. (1981) *Organization Development through Teambuilding*, Gower, Aldershot.

APPENDIX

Instruments used to Collect Evidence in the Evaluation of the Secondary Schools Management Programme discussed in Chapter 7.

(Instrument No. 1)

SECONDARY SCHOOL MANAGEMENT PROGRAMME:
QUESTIONNAIRE FOR LEA ADVISER

Your reply will be treated in the strictest confidence

---

1. **Background**

    a.   Your job title ....

    b.   Please list your responsibilities in respect of the programme:

2. **Selection**

    a.   How were participants selected?

    b.   Why were individual participants selected?

3. **Participants' Needs**

    a.   Please list up to three of the major needs of the participants
           that the programme is intended to address:

    ....

    ....

    ....

    b.   Indicate briefly how participants' needs were identified?

c.   Outline how participants' needs were communicated to the trainers:

4.   **Expectations**

Please give an outline of the LEA's expectations of the practical
outcomes of the programmes:

5.   **Follow-up**

What arrangements, if any, has the LEA made to provide follow-up
activities for the participants attending these programmes?

6.   **Group Leaders/Set Advisers**

How, if at all, does the LEA intend to make use in future
of the participants acting as group leaders/set advisers?

7.   **Any further comments you wish to make.**

(Instrument No. 2)

SECONDARY SCHOOL MANAGEMENT PROGRAMME:
OBSERVATION SCHEDULE FOR FIRST VISIT

Focus: any information relevant to:

    a.   how far the trainer's input meets participants' needs
    b.   the impact of the programme on participants' managerial practice in their institution.

Record: observations, quotations.

1. **Participants**

    a.   clarity about what expected of them

    b.   interest and motivation

    c.   proportion of time spent on task

    d.   interaction with other participants, including team leaders

    e.   interaction with trainer

    f.   perceived relevance of content to their practice

    g.   response to methods used by trainer

    h.   indication of actual and planned action in own institution

2. **Trainer**

    a.   attempt to identify and respond to participants' needs

    b.   preparation of room activities, materials, A.V. aids

    c.   sequencing of activities and use of time

    d.   communication of expectations of participants

    e.   communication of expectations of group leaders in this role

    f.   interaction with participants, including group leaders

    g.   attempt to relate content to participants' practice

    h.   attempt to use methods which will effectively promote learning

    i.   attempt to promote participants' actual and planned action in their own institution

3. **Unintended and Unanticipated Consequences**

    a.   positive developments

    b.   negative developments

(Summary of Instrument No. 3a)

SUMMARY OF SCHEDULE FOR INITIAL INTERVIEW WITH TRAINER

1:     What are the major needs of participants that you are trying to meet?

2.   How were these needs communicated to you?

3.   How, briefly, are you attempting to meet these needs?

4.   Are there any constraints or problems which are hampering your work?

5.   How effective are the group leaders in supporting your work?

6.   Do you have any recommendations to the programme director for improving the support for your work?

7.   Do you have any other comments?

(Summary of Instrument No. 3b)

SCHEDULE FOR INITIAL INTERVIEW WITH PROGRAMME DIRECTOR

1.   How were the reasons for selection communicated to those who volunteered to attend the programmes?

2.   How effective did you find the preparatory visits?

3.   How were the participants' needs communicated to the trainers?

4.   What, if any, are the major strengths of the trainers' work so far in meeting participants' needs?

5.   What, if any, are the major weaknesses of the trainers' work so far in meeting participants' needs?

6.   Do you have any recommendations to the trainers for improving their work in this or a future programme?

7.   How effective are the group leaders in supporting the trainers' work?

8.   What, if any, arrangements are planned so far for follow-up support of participants after the programmes are over?

9.   Do you have any other comments?

(Instrument No. 4)   Response No: ....

SECONDARY SCHOOL MANAGEMENT PROGRAMME:
INITIAL QUESTIONNAIRE FOR PARTICIPANTS

Your reply will be treated in the strictest confidence

For
Office
Use

1.   **Biographical Background**

    a.   Your name (optional) ....

    b.   Present position in school ....

    c.   Number of years in present post ....

2.   **Selection**

    a.   Please indicate briefly the process by which you were recruited
        to the programme:

    b.   Who, if anyone, informed you as to <u>why</u> you were selected to attend?

    ....

    c.   What reason for your selection, if any, was given?

3.   **Preparation**

    a.   Prior to the programme, you will have been offered the opportunity
        to meet the director, the trainers and other participants.

        If you took part in this meeting, how useful did you find this?

Very Useful   [   ] Quite Useful   [   ]   Not Very Useful   [   ]

    b.   Are there any recommendations you would like to put forward for
        making this meeting more effective?

c.   What modifications or additions, if any, would you recommend the
programme director to make to any written pre-programme information?

4.   **Individual Needs**

    a.   Please state up to three of your needs which you believe the programme
is intended to meet:

    i. ....

    ii. ....

    iii. ....

    b.   Please outline briefly how, if at all, your needs were identified
prior to the programme?

    c.   Outline briefly how, if at all, your needs have been identified so far
during the programme:

5.   **Expectations**

    a.   Please state up to three of your current expectations of the practical
outcomes of the programme:

    ....

    ....

    ....

    b.   How, if at all, were your LEA's expectations of the practical outcomes
of the programme communicated to you?

Off
L

c.   Please specify up to three of the LEA's expectations:

....

....

....

6.   **Statement of Problem** (optional)

If you wish, please give a brief outline of the statement of a problem
that you were asked to bring to the first part of the programme:

7.   **Individual Comments**

If you wish, please comment upon any aspect of your experience of the
programme so far. (Continue on another sheet if necessary)

Thank you for your help in completing this questionnaire.

(Instrument No. 5)

SECONDARY SCHOOL MANAGEMENT PROGRAMME:
ACTIVITY EVALUATION QUESTIONNAIRE

Module Number: ....

Title of activity: ....

Trainer's aims:

   i. ....

   ii. ....

   iii. ....

1.   How effective was each of the sessions in achieving the aims?

Session & focus	Aim	EFFECTIVENESS			Reasons for this judgement
		Very	Quite	Not	
1.					
2.					
3.					
4.					

2.   How, if at all, do you intend to make use in school of what you have learnt through this activity?

3.   Please make any suggestions about how this activity could be improved. (Please continue if necessary on the back of this sheet.)

_____

Thank you for your help. When you have finished, please hand this sheet to the trainer.

Response No. ....

SECONDARY SCHOOL MANAGEMENT PROGRAMME:
MID-PROGRAMME QUESTIONNAIRE FOR PARTICIPANTS

Your reply will be treated in the strictest confidence

Fo
Offic
Us

Biographical Background

    a.   Your name (optional) ....

    b.   Your present position in school ....

1.   **Overall Aim**

    a.   How effective has the programme offered by the trainers been so far in achieving the overall aim 'to improve the management, support and practice of the learning processes in schools'?

    very effective ☐   quite effective ☐   ineffective ☐

    b.   Please indicate briefly why you have come to this view on the effectiveness of the programme offered by the trainers so far in achieving the overall aim:

2.   **Groups**

    a.   How effective has the experience been so far of working in sets with a set adviser?

    very effective ☐   quite effective ☐   ineffective ☐

    b.   Please indicate why you have come to this view on the effectiveness of the experience of working in sets with a set adviser:

3. **Content**

   a. How effective has the programme content offered by the training been so far in:

      i. encouraging analysis of your role and managerial skills?
      ii. developing your confidence in using these managerial skills?
      iii. promoting networking within and between institutions?
      iv. promoting effective links with the local community?

PROGRAMME CONTENT	Encouraging Analysis			Developing Confidence			Promoting Networking			Promoting links with the local community		
	Very effective	Quite effective	Ineffective	Very effective	Quite effective	Ineffective	Very effective	Quite effective	Ineffective	Very effective	Quite effective	Ineffective
Clarifying roles and tasks												
Strategic Planning												
Managing LMS												
Managing the curriculum and assessment												
Managing staff development and appraisal												
Managing change												
The school in the community												
Building effective teams												
Marketing the school												
Other (please specify)												

b.   What modifications, if any, would you recommend the trainers to make to the programme content that you have experienced so far?

4.   **Methods**

a.   How effective have the methods or experiences offered by the trainers been so far in:

      i. encouraging analysis of your role and managerial skills?
      ii. developing your confidence in using these managerial skills?
      iii. promoting networking within and between institutions?
      iv. promoting effective links with the local community?

PROGRAMME METHODS	Encouraging analysis			Developing confidence			Promoting networks			Promoting links with local community		
	Very effective	Quite effective	Ineffective	Very effective	Quite effective	Ineffective	Very effective	Quite effective	Ineffective	Very effective	Quite effective	Ineffective
Preparatory tasks in school												
Presentation by trainers or visiting speakers												
Small group discussions												
Simulations and role play exercises												
Case studies												
Guided reading												
Skills training												
Action learning sets												
Visits to other schools												
Follow-up tasks in school												
Other (please specify):												

b.   What modifications, if any, would you recommend the trainers to make to the programme methods that you have experienced so far?

5.   **Impact of the Programme**

a.   Please indicate with which of your colleagues in your institution, if any, you have discussed changes that you have wished to initiate since attending the programme.

b.   Outline briefly what changes you have discussed.

c.   Give a brief outline of any changes you have made so far in your personal behaviour in your school as someone with managerial responsibility.

d.   Outline briefly any changes you have made so far in the management of your institution.

e.   Mention briefly any other development so far (intended or unintended) relating to you as a person or manager that has resulted from your attendance on the programme.

6.   **Organisation and General**

    a.

	Very effective	Quite effective	Ineffective
Please indicate how satisfactory you have found the following organisational aspects of the programme to be so far			
Location			
Time			
Financial arrangements, expenses, etc.			
Access to programme director			
Access to trainers			
Access to resources, books, materials, etc.			
Arrangements for visits			
Sequence of programme content			
Evaluation arrangements			
Other (please specify):			

    b.   What recommendations, if any, do you have for any modification of the organisation of the programme and its evaluation on the basis of your experience so far?

7.   If you wish, please comment on any aspect of the programme, such as its strengths and weaknesses (continue on another sheet if necessary).

(Instrument No. 7)   Response No. ....

SECONDARY SCHOOL MANAGEMENT PROGRAMME:
FINAL QUESTIONNAIRE FOR PARTICIPANTS

Your reply will be treated in the strictest confidence

	For Office Use

1. Biographical Background

a. Your name (optional) ....

b. Present position in school ....

c. Number of years in present post ....

2. Overall Aim

a.   How effective was the programme in achieving the overall aim
'to improve the management, support and practice of the
learning processes in schools'?

Very effective ☐   Quite effective ☐   Ineffective ☐

b.   Please indicate briefly why you have come to this view
on the effectiveness of the programme in achieving the overall aim:

c.   Did the programme meet your needs that you identified?

Yes ☐   Partly ☐   No ☐

Any comment on the extent to which the programme met your needs
that you identified:

3. **Content**

    a.   How effective was the programme content (e.g. personal skills, basic management theory) in:

	Very effective	Quite effective	Ineffective
1. encouraging analysis of your role and managerial skills?			
2. developing your confidence in using these managerial skills?			
3. promoting networking within and between institutions?			
4. promoting effective links with the local community?			

    b.   How effective was the programme in helping you to solve the problem that you were asked to bring to the first part of the programme?

Very effective [   ]   Quite effective [   ]   Ineffective [   ]

    c.   Please indicate why you have come to this view on the effectiveness of the programme in helping you to solve the problem:

4. **Methods**

    a.   How effective were the programme methods (e.g. action learning, presentations by the trainers) in:

	Very effective	Quite effective	Ineffective
1. encouraging analysis of your role and managerial skills?			
2. developing your confidence in using these managerial skills?			
3. promoting networking within and between institutions?			
4. promoting effective links with the local community			

b.   How effective was the experience of working in sets with
a set adviser?

Very effective   [   ]   Quite effective   [   ]   Ineffective   [   ]

Please indicate why you have come to this view on the effectiveness
of the experience of working in sets with a set adviser:

5.   **Impact of the Programme on you**

a.   What level of impact has the programme had upon your work
as a manager in school:

Major impact   [   ]   Some impact   [   ]   Little impact   [   ]

b.   Please indicate which of your colleagues in your
institution, if any, you have discussed the initiation of
any changes since the end of the programme:

c.   Outline briefly what changes you have discussed:

d.   Give a brief outline of any changes you have made since the programme
ended in your personal behaviour in your institution as someone
with managerial responsibility:

e.   Outline briefly any changes you have made since the end of the
programme in the management of your institution:

f.   Mention briefly any other development, whether intended or
        unintended, relating to you as a person or manager that has
        resulted from your attendance on the programme:

6.   **Impact on your colleague who attended the programme (optional)**

a.   Please indicate any changes that you have noticed in his or her
        personal behaviour that appears to be a result of attending
        one of the programmes (optional):

b.   Indicate briefly any changes you have noticed that he or she
        has made in the management of your institution that seems to
        have resulted from attending the programme (optional):

c.   Mention briefly any other development that you have noticed, intended
        or unintended, relating to him or her as a person or manager that
        that appears to have resulted from attending the programme (optional):

7.   **Follow-up Support**

a.   Please outline briefly what, if any, follow-up support you have received so
        far since the end of the programme from, for example, a colleague from
        your school who participated in the programme, other colleagues
        in school, another participant in the programme or an adviser:

b.   Indicate what, if any, follow-up support (and from whom) you
      expect in your role as manager of your institution in the
      coming year:

Improving Future Programmes

Please outline any changes that you may wish to recommend for
future programmes:

a.   the process of selection and preparation:

b.   trainers for the programme:

c.   programme content:

d.   programme methods:

e. programme organisation (e.g. venue, access to resources, evaluation arrangements):

f. follow-up support after the programme:

9. **Individual comments**

If you wish, please comment upon any aspect of the programme, such as its strengths and weaknesses (continue on another sheet if necessary).

Thank you for your help in completing this questionnaire.
Please send it in the prepaid envelope provided to (name of evaluator, address) by Friday, 24th May, 1991.

(Instrument No. 8)

SUMMARY OF IMPACT INTERVIEW SCHEDULE

Participant's name: ....

Role (head, deputy, set adviser): ....

1. Strengths of the programme

2. Weaknesses of the programme

3. Effectiveness of trainers (including methods, relevance of inputs, variety)

4. Effectiveness of action learning sets (including role of set adviser, solving management problem)

5. **For set advisers only** - preparation, effectiveness, problems as set advisers, recommendations for future

6. Effect of head and deputy attending same programme   (including impact on head and deputy relationship)

7. Impact of programme:

    o   personal   awareness/knowledge
                     skills
                     attitudes
                     performance in school (including solving management problem)

    o   on colleagues in school   outcome of discussion
                                    outcome of behaviour

8. Impact of process of evaluation (including distraction, workload)

9. Recommendations for improvements in programme and process of:

         selection
         preparation
         follow-up

10. Any other comments

INDEX